Follow the Leader
Discover the Dynamic Journey of Discipleship

Bill Sytsma

PublishAmerica
Baltimore

© 2006 by Bill Sytsma.
All rights reserved. No part of this book may be reproduced, stored in a retrieval system or transmitted in any form or by any means without the prior written permission of the publishers, except by a reviewer who may quote brief passages in a review to be printed in a newspaper, magazine or journal.

First printing

At the specific preference of the author, PublishAmerica allowed this work to remain exactly as the author intended, verbatim, without editorial input.

ISBN: 1-4241-5560-6
PUBLISHED BY PUBLISHAMERICA, LLLP
www.publishamerica.com
Baltimore

Printed in the United States of America

Dedication

For my parents, Don and Marcia Sytsma:
thank-you for leading me to Christ.

Acknowledgments

When I first sat down to try and write a book, I was completely unaware of the process that would transform my ideas into a published book. I owe a great debt of gratitude to many people who helped me with that process.

To my wife, Staci: thank-you for your constant encouragement and support. I am blessed to have you as my wife, and I am thankful for your willingness to discuss ideas and help me find the right phrases to communicate those thoughts. I thank God for bringing us together, and I pray that He will help us lead our children to follow Christ.

To my sister, Bonnie Stephens: thank you for being the first person willing to read the manuscript for this book. Your kind words encouraged me to keep going.

To my mentor and friend, David Deters: thank you for helping me to think carefully about how I use words and illustrations to communicate God's truth.

To my coworker and friend, Ray Haan: thank you for careful work to edit this book. I appreciated your thoughtful efforts to help me communicate clearly.

To the congregation of Cutlerville East Christian Reformed Church: thank you for the time you allowed me to write, and for your willingness to listen to many sermons that helped me clarify the concepts in this book.

It is my hope and prayer that this book will help many to grow closer to God and bring Him glory.

Table of Contents

I. Understanding the Image of Following:
Chapter 1: Who Wants to Follow? 7
Chapter 2: Christians Are Followers 13
Chapter 3: We Have a Leader 26
Chapter 4: Push Through the Pain 37
Chapter 5: Peak Performance Requires Total Commitment 55
Chapter 6: Chasing Your Tail: The Futility of Following Yourself 73
Chapter 7: Playing Copycat 87
Chapter 8: The Metamorphosis of the Chase 103
Chapter 9: Blending into the Crowd 117

II. Learning from the Original Followers
Chapter 10: Peter: Bold and Prone to Stumble 131
Chapter 11: John: The Beloved Disciple 139
Chapter 12: Thomas: Faithful Pessimist 148
Chapter 13: Judas Iscariot: Rebellion 158
Chapter 14: Paul: A Turnaround Story 167
Chapter 15: The Unheralded Crowd 176
Chapter 16: Catch the Vision 184

Bibliography 191
Endnotes 195

Chapter 1
Who Wants to Follow?

This book is about following Christ.

That opening line probably does not sound too thrilling. If you are like most people, you do not want to be known as a "follower." You probably think that following is a boring, mundane activity, and you can think of much better ways to spend your time. Following other people means that we are subject to their whims, and that we must bend our lives in order to accommodate them.

If it were up to me, I would like to choose a word other than "follower" to describe my relationship with Christ. Other Biblical images, such as born-again believers,[1] fishers of men,[2] or soldiers of the cross,[3] are much more dynamic and interesting descriptions of a Christian lifestyle. I would like to be a leader, or even a servant,[4] in Christ's church who uses his spiritual gifts[5] to bear fruit.[6] But I must confess that I do not quickly warm up to the idea of being called a follower.

Despite my hesitancy to be called a follower, Christ used the term regularly to identify His disciples. The first and last commandment that Christ gave to His disciples in the Gospels is "follow me."[7] In this book, we will consider the fullness of that commandment. I hope that by the end of this book we are able to look beyond the negative connotations of following in order to see that a life of following Christ is a dynamic journey of realizing the full potential that God created in us.

The Same Game

When my children were young, I spent years playing the same game over and over. I called it "Catch me, if you can." The object of the game was to pursue my children. This game had a variety of names. Sometimes we called it tag or chase, other times we called it hide-and-go-seek or the catch and wrestle game. This game also began in a number of different ways. Sometimes my kids would taunt me as they beckoned with a mocking cadence, "Na-na, you can't get me," other times they would start with a question, "Daddy, will you chase me?" or with a statement, "Tag, you're it!" Regardless of the name or the way the game started it was basically the same game.

If you had told me when I was in college that I was going to spend years playing one game with my children, I would have scoffed. Playing the same game over and over would have seemed like a boring life, lacking imagination and creativity. Yet I have been pleasantly surprised to discover that playing the same game has its advantages. As I play, I become less concerned about the process or the game, and I begin to know more and more about my children. The game becomes nothing more than a tool for relating to them as a father.

Like a father who plays the same game with his children, Christians face a lifetime of what may appear to be an interminable process of following Christ. The prospect of this lifestyle may cause some to turn up their noses, but as we move forward in a life of following, we begin to realize that a life of following is far from boring and mundane. It is life filled with the joys of seeing God complete His work in us.

Christ calls us to join Him in a dynamic journey of realizing the potential that He created in each one of us. He may call with a challenge, or invite us to join Him for a time of comforting encouragement, or even rebuke us for leaving Him. The way He calls each of us may differ from person to person, but He desires the same response from each of us. He wants us to follow Him.

The Response of Following

How do we respond to the call of Christ?

In my life I have gone to extremes in my response to Christ's call. Sometimes I have taken a minimalist approach. I have read texts that say, "Believe in the Lord Jesus, and you will be saved,"[8] and "We maintain that a man is justified by faith apart from observing the law."[9] In response to these kinds of statements, I have reasoned that all I needed to do was intellectually believe what the Bible said, and I would be acceptable in God's eyes. I thought this was a rather freeing concept. According to this line of thought, I had no obligations about how I lived my life. My only obligation was to believe. How those beliefs affected my life was a question that never needed to be considered.

This approach led me to an empty walk with God. I may have believed what the Bible said, but I experienced little or no joy. To be honest, I did not even have a very strong sense of assurance that I was saved.

Because of this emptiness, I may have overreacted. I still believed that Jesus saved me, but my response changed. I read passages that said, "Be Holy because I am Holy,"[10] and "A person is justified by what he does and not by faith alone."[11] I realized that responding to Christ meant more than merely believing a set of intellectual propositions. God wanted me to be like Him. I was called to be perfect.

As a result of my new response, I did indeed strive very hard to be like Jesus. I wanted to be perfect. I held no illusion that my own actions could save me, but I had to strive. I discovered moments of joy as I responded to God in this way. But, I also experienced a high level of frustration.

I am competitive by nature. I like setting personal goals. If I do not reach those goals, I believe I have failed. In my striving to be perfect and holy, I fell short. As a result, I became frustrated in my walk with God.

Perhaps you have struggled with similar thoughts. Maybe you have realized that God wants more from you than merely believing that He is real. Maybe you have set goals for yourself to keep all of God's commandments perfectly, and you realize that you have fallen short.

Jesus often told His disciples to, "Follow Me." In this phrase, I found the guidance I needed to respond to the good news of Jesus.

Do you remember playing the game, "Follow the leader?" It was a simple game in principle. The object of the game was to imitate, as closely as you could, whatever the leader did. I can remember long lines of friends marching around school playgrounds. When the leader hopped on one foot, all those behind her did the same. When the leader flapped her arms like a chicken, a line full of chickens flapped, too. The game appeared to have no object. No one was ever declared a winner or a loser. It was simply enjoyable to do what the leader was doing.

Who would have thought that a simple children's game could be used to teach us something about our walk with God? Our response to the call of Christ is to follow Him. We are to imitate Him and to obey His commands. In that process of following we find incredible blessings of peace and security.

When I am leading a worship service, I frequently refer to Christians as "followers of Christ." I do this, because it describes how Christians respond to Christ. We are followers of Christ who carry out His work and imitate Him. We rely on His grace for our eternal salvation.

It is hard to describe what it means to be a Christian. During Jesus' ministry, He often used parables to describe His Kingdom. In these parables we find a number of word pictures to describe Christians. We are like lost sheep who have been found, runaway children who have come home, servants who have been given authority, convicted criminals who have been declared innocent, and debtors who have been released from their obligation. Yet in each of those parables, we are defined by what God has done for us. He found us, welcomed us home, gave us authority, and forgave our debts. We are saved because of what God did for us in Christ. However, we are not called to be passive recipients. We receive the gift freely, but it is not without effect in our lives. Therefore, how do we respond to Christ's work? In an attempt to answer that question, I want to consider one of the most frequent commands of Jesus. "Follow Me."

When Jesus began His ministry, He told His twelve companions that they should follow Him[12]. Those twelve were called disciples. The word disciple does not really have a contemporary equivalent, but it is tied very closely to the idea of following. A disciple was bound to his teacher or master, learned from his master, and desired to be like his master. A disciple was more than a student or a pupil; he was committed to follow where his master led.

Disciple = Student + Follower

Perhaps the best way to approach the concept of discipleship is to perceive how the concept differs from our common view of what it means to be a student.

When I was in high school and college, I was privileged to learn from many wonderful teachers. I appreciated what many of them had to teach me, but my fondness and appreciation never developed to the point that I wanted to be like them. I was a student, willing to submit myself to their teaching. This meant that I would willingly write papers, take tests, and show up for scheduled class times. Nevertheless, my willingness had firm limits: I was not going to follow my teachers blindly. Regardless of my admiration for them, I was not going to let my teachers govern my love life nor my choice of friends.

When Christ called people to be His disciples, He was calling them to a deeper kind of commitment. Even though He called them to be His students, and He helped them understand truths about the Kingdom of God; a disciple was more than a mere student. A disciple followed. Christ's disciples traveled with Him, submitted to Him, and imitated Him. Christ did not allow for any limits in their commitment to Him or His teaching. He called His followers to abandon their families and friends so that they could pursue Him.[13]

As contemporary Christians, we would benefit from seeing ourselves as followers of Christ. The concept of following is still our model for responding to Christ's call. Before Jesus ascended into heaven, He told His followers that they were to go and make disciples.[14] In this final command, Jesus indicates that His program of discipleship is to continue. His followers were assigned to go and make fellow followers.[15] Viewing ourselves as followers helps us realize that we are works in progress. It grants us reassurance that there is Someone Who is leading us.

In this book, I want to invite you to join me in a lifelong journey of following Christ. He has called us to pursue Him. I like to think of it as attempting to "catch" Him, even though I know that I will never really accomplish that. However, this book will not be a step-by-step program for growing in Christ. Instead, I hope to convince you that following Christ is the best image for us to keep in mind as we live in relationship with Him. I also hope to point out some of the landmarks of the journey, so that we can see how our pursuit of Christ changes us to be more like Him. In the final section of this book I will point out how some of the landmarks of following Christ were evident in the lives of His first followers.

Questions for discussion/reflection:

What do you think of someone who is called a follower? Is it a positive image?

Why would someone say the Christian life is boring? Is this a fair statement?

Do you think more Christians struggle to be perfectionists, or try to get by doing as little as they can (the minimalist approach)? Which extreme have you struggled with?

Which people have been role models for you? Parents? Extended Family? Teachers? Coaches? How have you followed or imitated them with your life?

Chapter 2
Christians Are Followers

Salvation is God's work.

If you are a Christian, your hope for salvation rests completely in what God has done for you. He created you, sent His Son, Jesus, to die for you, and He continually guides you by His Holy Spirit. Salvation is His responsibility. It is His inexpressibly marvelous gift to you.

The New Testament tells us a great deal about God's work to save His people. Jesus' parables are brief explanations of what God's Kingdom is like. In these stories we see many descriptions of God's actions to save His people.

God is like a master who forgives a debt.[16] He is like a father who anxiously awaits the return of his prodigal son.[17] He is like a king who eagerly welcomes anyone to a great feast for his son.[18] These stories wonderfully describe our God and what He has done for us.

Once we realize that salvation is God's work, the next logical question is this: "What do I have to do?" It is a fair question because we want to be faithful in our response to One who was so kind and gracious as to save us.

Occasionally, I have fallen into the trap of believing that I must earn God's saving grace. I have followed a disciplined regimen in order to uphold God's law to the best of my ability, and my efforts have led to frustration. Inevitably, I have discovered that I will never be good enough to earn God's salvation. I have been relieved by my burden of self-righteousness whenever I have remembered that God has already given me the gift of salvation. I have to constantly remind myself that salvation is God's work. My response does not make me "more saved," even though my response can put me in a position to have greater joy in that salvation.

At other times, I have searched for tangible evidence that I have been saved. I have been convinced of my salvation based on the fact that I said a particular prayer, or because I have professed my belief in the Bible, or even because I could point to a time when I had a highly-charged religious or emotional experience. Although I am grateful for these experiences, these responses fall short of Christ's call to follow.

"Follow me is the substance of the call"[19] that Jesus makes in our lives. He does not expect us to be perfect, for He was perfect in our place. On the other hand, He never indicates that we can slide by with a minimum commitment to Him.

Jesus' call to follow offers a full and balanced picture of the response that He requires of Christians. Though that response is within our reach, it does not pacify our consciences with an easy, one-time obligation. His call is hard because it requires our very life; yet it is comforting because as we follow Him, we travel under His protection and come at last to share in His victory.

In this chapter we will take a close look at the responses that fall short of Christ's call to follow Him. Those who think a religious experience or a simple belief is all that Christ requires miss the fullness of His call.

Devon's Question

In the summer of 1991 I worked with Devon, a bricklayer. It was obvious that Devon loved the Lord. He would often quote scripture passages to explain the reasons for his behavior. Many Christians quote scripture passages in a way that seems to be born of pride. Not Devon. He had a sincerity that drew others nearer to him.

Devon heard from someone on the jobsite that I was studying to become a minister. After hearing this, he sought me out. He wanted to encourage me and to discuss our common faith in Christ. After hearing about my church background, the school I was attending, and how I came to believe that God wanted me to be a pastor, Devon asked a question that struck me as rather odd, "What is your spiritual birthday?"

I understood what Devon was asking. As a born-again Christian, he wanted to know the specific date of my conversion. When I told him that I did not know the specific date, he became very concerned. The enthusiasm in his eyes faded as he looked down at the ground and said in a low, despondent voice, "That's too bad."

"Why?" I innocently asked.

"Because, if you were really born again, you should remember your birthday. It was an important day."

I tried to share the story of my faith with Devon. I explained to him that I could not remember a time when I did not believe that God was real. I shared with him how my parents had taught me to pray. I even told him that as a teenager I had made a conscious decision to follow Christ, not just because it was a family tradition, but because I believed that Jesus loved me and that He died for me. This was no consolation to Devon. He was convinced that since I could not point to a time when I experienced a radical spiritual rebirth, he had reason to doubt the sincerity of my faith.

I understand the reason for Devon's concern. I fear that far too many people have fallen into Christianity and church attendance as a matter of family tradition. I fear that many who can recite the ten commandments, the Lord's Prayer, and Psalm 23 have never given serious consideration to what the grace of Jesus Christ means for their lives. Too many believe they are righteous in God's eyes, yet they have never confessed their sins and asked for the saving grace of Christ to alter the course of their lives.

In John 3 the Bible tells us the story of Nicodemus, a religious leader of the Jews who knew all the right things. Though he understood the law and had read the prophecies of the Old Testament, something in his life caused him to seek out Jesus under the dark of night. He wanted to understand how it could be that Jesus performed so many signs and miracles.

Jesus always cut to the heart of the matter. Instead of dealing with theoretical debates about signs and miracles, Jesus told Nicodemus that if he wanted to see the Kingdom of God, he needed to be born again. That statement stunned Nicodemus. He wanted to know how he could enter into his mother's womb a second time. In a way, I can sympathize with Nicodemus. This must have been very strange language for him. He started the conversation very politely, probably not expecting it to get so personal.

Today we have had years of Christian history to help us understand what Jesus said. When Christ comes, He gives us new life. When we submit to Christ as Lord and Savior, newness drowns out the old way of living. We live to please Christ rather than ourselves. The old priorities fade into obscurity as we are filled with the joy and contentment that nothing can separate us from eternity in our Master's presence.

Many Christians have dramatic testimonies about changes in their lives once they prayed that Christ would save them. In his book, Dealer, Jon Kregel tells how his life changed once he asked Christ to rule in his heart. The son of missionary parents, and a Bible school graduate, Jon had been a professional soccer player, a night club entertainer, a cocaine addict, and a convicted criminal.[20] After his arrest and conviction Jon remembered the lessons of his youth and asked Christ into His life. Even in prison his life began to change. After his release from prison, Jon began to speak to high school students about his experiences. He found many opportunities to share the good news of Jesus with students who were lost and searching. Jon experienced a profound spiritual rebirth.

I used to envy people like Jon. I loved hearing testimonies about people whose lives were turned upside down by Christ. Still, I often felt inferior as a Christian, because I did not have a dramatic story of my life being turned around after a watershed moment of recognizing Christ for the first time. I could never point to myself as an example of one who had been taken from the pits and brought into glory.

Devon wanted to know how my life had been radically altered by Christ on a specific day. My inability to name one particular day dismayed him, but that did not mean I was lost. Even though I could not recall a specific date, I could say with confidence that Christ had altered the direction of my life. It is not necessary to know your spiritual birthday in order to be a follower of Christ.

An Instant or a Process?

Jesus told Nicodemus that one must be "born again" to enter the Kingdom of Heaven. I believe that this is absolutely true. I hear many people describe themselves as "born again" Christians. I appreciate the description, because it is from the Bible. I am pleased that people want others to know that they have experienced the grace of Christ. I am glad that people believe their lives have been radically altered by Jesus.

However, I am concerned about relating spiritual rebirth only to a one time event. Christians are not defined by one-time events. Jesus said, "I am the Way."[21] He did not say, "I am the door."[22] Life in Christ means we are on a long journey. If we focus on the initial experience of coming to acknowledge Christ as our Savior, we might be missing what God has yet to accomplish in our lives.

When I was younger, I would question the sincerity of my faith, because I never had what I would have described as a radical moment of instantaneously realizing how far I was from God and how much I needed Him. I would hear stories of men and women who had been on a path to self-destruction. They would tell of a particular moment in their lives when they were awakened to the reality of God's grace. They were convinced that their lifestyles were leading to emptiness, and they began the journey of following Jesus.

When I heard these stories, I felt envy. I wanted a moment when my life was changed. I even wondered whether my spiritual life would benefit from walking away from God for a while so that He could rescue me in a miraculous manner. I wanted the "born-again" moment that Devon had asked me about. In time, I came to realize that the Christian life is not defined by a moment of insight, but it is marked by a journey of following Jesus.

Spiritual rebirth happens in an instant. Following Christ takes a lifetime. You might remember the beauty of the moment when you first realized that you needed Christ. The joy of that moment may still bring tears to your eyes. However, the totality of your walk with God is not contained in that momentary experience. He has much more to do with you; it takes a lifetime to live out the acknowledgment that you are forgiven and saved from the consequences of sin.

I remember my wedding day with fondness. The ceremony was a moment that changed the direction of my life. When I walked into the Judson College Chapel on a November day in 1993, I was a single man, able to take my life in the direction I wanted to go. A couple hours later I was married, and from that moment my path in life was intertwined with my wife. I then had to consider more than my desires; I had to consider hers as well. Though the moment of marriage changed my legal and social status, it did not define me as a faithful husband. Many couples enter a church, chapel, or courtroom with sincere intentions of being faithful to their wedding vows. Sadly, many of those sincere people go on to break their vows. Even if they felt a great moment of love and joy as their wedding vows were made, they do not remain faithful.

Similarly, God calls His people to be faithful to Him. Followers of Christ might experience wonderfully blissful moments. Those blissful moments, however, do not define a person's walk with God. We are called to follow Christ.

Following Christ is a life-long process. It involves taking off the old self and putting on the new self.[23] It requires that we focus our eyes on Jesus, and therefore it changes the way we live.

In Matthew 24 Jesus speaks about the final judgment day. On that day Jesus will separate humanity into two groups, those who are saved and those who are condemned. Each group, He says, will ask why they were given their placement. Jesus will not respond by asking people about their spiritual birthdays. He will not ask people to tell about a particular experience in their lives, for the evidence of faith in Christ cannot be reduced to one-time experiences. Rather it appears in a life of following Jesus. Jesus will tell those who are saved that they have shared their possessions with others and comforted those in need. He will point out that their faith has been evident in their actions: they have followed Him. The criterion will be whether or not they have followed

Christ. Their religious experiences affected the stories of their lives.

A Lesson from the Great Awakening

Devon's question caused me to question the sincerity of my faith. Because of his doubt, I started to wonder whether I needed to have a mystical religious experience in order to be truly saved. Years later, I was pleasantly surprised to discover that I was not the first person who had ever wondered about the value of religious experiences.

In the eighteenth century Jonathan Edwards was one of America's leading pastors and theologians. During his ministry, there was a great deal of discussion about true religious experiences. It was a time of revival meetings. Itinerant preachers traveled in rural areas and hosted meetings that often resulted in mysterious and frenzied religious phenomena. Stories were told of great religious fervor, deeply moving experiences, and unbridled praise at these gatherings.

In his book, The Religious Affections,[24] Edwards addressed the question of determining whether mysterious experiences were truly from God. Edwards spent a great deal of time describing religious experiences that are characterized by excitement, joy, fluency, zeal, expression of praise, and moving testimonies. He concluded that these characteristics are ambiguous. They might be born out of truly religious experiences, but they are not reliable signs that God has worked miraculously in someone's life. Religious fervor can be wonderful, but it is not a reliable indicator of a person's faith. Edwards did not deny that highly emotional religious experiences might be real. He did, however, say that these phenomena should not be accepted as true and good without any critical analysis. Even if these phenomena are accompanied by quotations from scripture and by moving testimonies and expressions of praise, we cannot be immediately certain that they are from God.

Edwards concluded The Religious Affections by arguing that true faith can be seen in the way a person lives his or her life. The practice of our faith in our daily living is the surest sign that religious affections are truly from God. Moments of joy can be wonderful, but the proof is in the practice. The way followers of Christ live testifies to God's work in their lives.

Edward's reflections on faith and religious experiences were a great comfort to me. He helped me realize that a one-time religious experience is not a prerequisite for true faith, and he argued that true faith can best be seen in the way a person lives. His thoughts convinced me that the best indicator of true faith is a lifestyle that is directed to following Christ.

Jolene's Story[25]

God can, and often does, reveal Himself in incredible ways.

Jolene DeHeer's life is an example of God's power to change a life through a miraculous revelation. In her early life, Jolene endured a number of struggles. She felt distant from her family, lacked a positive self image, and needed confidence.

If you met Jolene today, however, you would be amazed. She is a wonderfully vibrant person with a powerful speaking ministry. She seems just as at home leading a rally for rowdy teenagers as she does conducting a prayer meeting. Her wonderfully unique combination of gifts enables her to cause an audience to roar with laughter one moment, and to be silent with awe in God's presence in the next.

Jolene gives a testimony of a life-changing moment. One evening Jolene took many pills in an attempt to end her life. When the overdose of medication was beginning to affect her, she had a vision. She saw Jesus standing in the room with her, reaching to her with outstretched arms. At once Jolene realized that she did not want to die. Miraculously, God spared her life that evening.

Before I tell you more about Jolene, it might be worthwhile to stop at this point in the story. Many people might want to raise questions about her vision that night. Was Jesus really, physically in the room with her? Couldn't her vision have been a result of the medication? Does Jesus ever appear in that manner any more? Could God have given her a vision of Jesus without the physical presence of Jesus? There are probably many possible ways to try to explain what Jolene actually saw that night. When I first heard the story, I was skeptical myself. Today, however, I feel no need to doubt that God worked in some powerful way that evening.

I do not say that because I believe that visions of Jesus are common occurrences. I say that because I have seen how God is using Jolene. Today, she runs a ministry[26] in which she speaks to varied groups on varied topics about God's love, and how it encompasses our lives. God has used her to touch many lives.

I want to suggest that testimonies of wonderful revelations or profound religious experiences are indeed possible. We know from scripture that God has often worked in profoundly mysterious and remarkable ways.

For example, Moses experienced God's presence in a miraculous way when he spoke to a burning bush.[27] Mary, the mother of Jesus, was visited by an angel.[28] Samuel, a young boy living in the temple heard the voice of God speak to him during the night.[29] Saul, a one time persecutor of the church, encountered Jesus in a vision on the road to Damascus.[30] Each of these persons received a miraculous revelation from God. We believe that these accounts are true because we read about them in scripture. These revelations changed lives. These experiences were only the beginning of a process that God was working in the lives of these people.

So, profound and mysterious religious experiences are not the complete extent of God's call in our lives. He does not reveal Himself to His people in wonderful ways so that we can recall a single emotional experience. These profound experiences are merely the beginning of His work to transform us into followers of Christ.

The proof of God's work in Jolene's life is not her testimony that she saw Jesus one evening. The proof is that she is following Him and being used by Him today. The question of Christ's physical presence might be interesting to debate, but it seems almost certain that God worked in some way that night. His work began a process of transforming Jolene's life.

God's work in our lives is intended to bring more than an instant emotional experience. It is intended to bring us a new life. That new life enfolds us as we follow Him. If we are looking for emotional experiences to be the proof of our faith, we are missing the call that Christ gave us.

We began with Devon's question and my doubts relating to my lack of a dramatic testimony. It should be clear now that I no longer doubt my faith, simply because I cannot recall my spiritual birthday. Living a life of faith is not limited to a momentary experience. Christ calls us into a process of following Him.

More than Belief

At the relatively young age of 42, Darin experienced a massive heart attack. When I first met Darin, a couple of years after he had recovered from that attack, he explained how that experience changed his life. He told me, "I used to believe, but after my heart attack, I'm a follower!" Darin's statement demonstrated that he realized there is a difference between merely believing what the Bible says, and following Christ.

Simple belief and true belief are two different concepts. Simple belief is nothing more than intellectual agreement. When I say that I believe the world is round, I am expressing a simple belief. My belief does not call for any kind of response. Many people think simply believing that God is real is enough, and it is true that the Bible tells us that we must believe in Christ to be saved.[31] True belief, however, will change our lives. True belief is more than simply agreeing with a statement. True belief calls us to act out our beliefs, compels us to live in newness of life, and alters our view of the world around us.

The book of James helps us understand that the concepts of faith and believing are incomplete if we look at them too simply. James tells us, "You believe that there is one God? Good! Even the demons believe that—and shudder."[32] Christ is not calling us to simple belief. He wants us to enjoy the fullness of a relationship with Himself. In order for us to do that, we must submit ourselves completely. We must submit our minds, our wills, and even our actions. That same chapter in James tells us, "faith by itself, if it is not accompanied by action, is dead."[33] James is telling us that true belief in Christ will naturally move us to a new way of living.

Belief is necessary. It is even a good first step in following Christ. But it is an incomplete response.

Tom's Belief

Tom was a beginning investor in the stock market, and his friend Ryan was his broker. Tom had seen Ryan's wealth increase in the time that he was a broker.

One Monday morning, Tom received a call from Ryan.

"Tom, I have found a can't-miss stock that you should buy. I have sold every stock I own to invest in this one. I have legally acquired information that makes me certain that this stock is going to triple in value in the next two weeks."

Tom was not a very aggressive investor, so he hesitated in his response.

"I'm not sure, Ryan. It sounds kind of risky."

"Of course there's a risk, Tom. But I'm telling you that this stock can't miss. It will triple, maybe quadruple, in a very short period of time. If you want to act, you must do so quickly."

"Let me think about it, Ryan. I'll call you back in thirty minutes."

Tom hesitated. It seemed scary to put money into something without being completely sure of what would happen.

As he considered the prospect, he realized that he did indeed trust Ryan's integrity. Moreover, Ryan had done very well in the stock market. He believed that the information Ryan received was probably reliable and he trusted Ryan's instincts.

Believing was one thing. Acting was another.

Despite his belief, Tom decided not to invest. He felt too uncertain about the whole process, and didn't like that uncertainty. He did not return Ryan's call that day.

Two weeks later, he decided to call Ryan back.

"Ryan, for the past two weeks I have been thinking about that stock you called me about. I believed what you said, but I just didn't have the nerve to call you back. How has that stock been performing?"

"Tom, I was wrong. The stock did not triple. Instead, it went up by a factor of ten. I really wish you had acted and called me."

Tom had believed, but he did not allow that belief to alter his actions.

Tom's dilemma is similar to that of many who believe good things about Christ but are unwilling to follow Him. They might believe the Bible, they might have positive thoughts about Jesus, and they might even believe that He is Lord. But they are unwilling to act on what they believe.

Acting on that belief would not earn them salvation, for salvation is God's work. However, acting on that belief would enable them to benefit from Christ's work.

Belief is a good start, but it is not the fulfillment of Christ's call, which is to follow Him. True faith will naturally swell into the way we live our lives, changing our actions. True faith will lead us to follow Christ.

Have I Gone Too Far?

There is a danger in speaking of faith and of following Christ in this manner. Whenever someone speaks of the connection between faith and action, others might conclude that the only way we are saved is by our deeds. I want do dispel that idea right now. Our good behavior will not earn our salvation. We are saved only because of what Jesus Christ has done for us, His followers. If we were left to our own devices, we could never satisfy God's requirements to be in His presence. Because of Christ, we do not have to. He was perfectly righteous and voluntarily suffered the wrath of God so that His followers would not have to. We receive the gift of salvation because we have faith in Him, not because our works are good enough to earn salvation.

True faith, however, will naturally change our actions, giving evidence that faith is real. This is why the Bible tells us that faith and actions are inseparable, and why the Bible tells us that true religion results in a new way of living.[34] We may experience a momentary conversion, or we may come to know Christ by a slow process; either way, our response must be to follow Him. Christians are born again to follow their Leader.

Being a follower of Christ is a full picture of what God wants from us. He works in our lives to save us, and He then calls us to Himself. We do not satisfy the demands of His call by remembering one moment nor by intellectually believing that the Bible is true. The call is to follow Christ.

Now that we have discussed the fullness of the concept of following Christ, we will turn our attention in the next chapter to the One we follow. We will see that He is worth following.

Questions for discussion/reflection:

Do you remember the first time you prayed that Christ would be your Savior?

When have you had a moment, or period of time, that you consider a "spiritual high"? Do you believe that moment was genuine? How did that moment change your life?

Do you call yourself a "born-again" Christian? Why or why not?

Is your walk with God a momentary experience or a process? Explain.

How will sincere belief affect a person's life?

Chapter 3
We Have a Leader

What difference does it really make?

This is the question I ask every time my family decides to purchase a different vehicle. After the adoption of our second child, my wife and I decided to purchase a minivan. I read reports and looked at brochures, comparing the Dodge, Chrysler, Chevrolet, Ford, Mercury, Plymouth, and Toyota. After looking at different features, comparing prices, and talking to mechanics, I came to the conclusion that there were almost no differences among those vehicles.

To some people this may seem like heresy. I know vehicle owners who will swear that their Ford (or Dodge or Chevy) is the only reliable means of transportation that has ever been built. Some people do have stylistic preferences for particular makes and models of vehicles. But for the most part, there is very little difference. They all run on a petroleum based fuel and carry about the same number of passengers.

Even though I am a Christian, I must confess that there were times in my life when I have wondered, "Why do I believe Christ is the only hope for salvation? Could it be that Christianity is just one of many valid religions?" I questioned whether choosing a religion is like choosing a vehicle. After all, most religions prescribe a code of laws for conducting our lives, challenge us, and help us to set priorities. I wondered whether all of these common characteristics were evidence that there are no significant differences among the major world religions.

Is choosing a religion anything more than an exercise of finding a system of teaching that best fits their lifestyle? Why do Christians believe that we must follow Christ? Is there something unique about Him that makes Christianity unique? Is there a reason we should give His teaching more credibility than the teaching of Muhammad or Buddha?

As I struggled with these questions, I began to consider the uniqueness of Christ. I looked at the stories of His ministry in the Bible, and found some helpful insights from Christians like Charles Colson and C.S. Lewis that convinced me that Jesus is the only person worth following with our entire lives.

Beyond Admirable

The world has seen many noteworthy leaders and teachers. Many have inspired crowds, and some are reported to have performed miraculous signs. Still, Jesus is arguably the most admired person in the history of the world. Even people who are not Christians look to Jesus as an inspirational character. Hindus, Buddhists, Muslims, and even Jewish people admire Him as a religious leader and teacher.[35] What other person who lived 2,000 years ago appears regularly on the cover of Newsweek magazine?[36] Clearly, you do not have to be a Christian to admire Jesus, nor must you be born again to believe that Jesus was a great teacher. Christians, though, believe that Jesus is the One that we should follow. Why is this so?

Christians believe that Jesus was more than a great man. He was God in the flesh, living a life of perfect submission to the Father, and upholding all of the laws and commandments. He loved us enough to go to the cross and pay for our sin. Finally, because He is God and because He has conquered sin and death, He has all authority in heaven and on earth.[37]

If we are going to respond to Christ's salvation by following Him, we should be convinced that He is worth following. As we examine the uniqueness of His life and ministry and see the love and power He demonstrated for us, we begin to understand that He is worth following with our full devotion.

Authoritative Ministry

Jesus demonstrated authority in His ministry that is unparalleled by any other leader or teacher. Early in Christ's ministry, that authority[38] marked Him as being different. At first glance, it may seem as if Christ's authority was mere confidence. When He taught, He did not rely on other teachers or leaders to agree with Him. At one point in His ministry Christ explained that He did not need the approval of other men because He had the testimony of the Father.[39] The first time I studied this passage, it struck me as rather odd. Jesus seemed to be acting in a way that was inconsistent with His own teaching. He encouraged His followers to be humble servants, and yet in this passage he demonstrated a great deal of what the Jews called "chutzpah."[40] He scorned the idea that he needed other humans to testify on His behalf. His testimony was supported by the Father, and that was sufficient.

Christ's boldness could be confused with human arrogance. But there is a tremendous difference. Jesus had no reason to speak with arrogance. He was not looking for human approval. When the people tried to crown Him King, he refused.[41] When He had the opportunity to avoid the suffering of the cross, He refused.[42] Jesus' boldness about Himself was not a ploy to impress those around Him, it was an attempt to help them understand His role in their salvation.

Those who argue that Jesus' authority can be understood as mere confidence fail to recognize that there was more evidence that points to His uniqueness. His personal authority was observed in His miracles.

The Bible tells of other humans who performed wonderful miracles. For example, Elijah brought the people of Israel to the top of Mt. Carmel for a great contest between the true God of Israel and the false gods, Baal and Asherah.[43] Elijah arranged the exhibition to demonstrate the power of the one true God over the false gods. He began by instructing the prophets of Baal and Asherah to prepare an offering and then summon their gods to send fire to burn it. Hundreds of prophets screamed to their gods for hours, begging them to send fire. Elijah sat calmly on the side, mocking them by suggesting that their gods were on a bathroom break and by encouraging them to shout louder. After enough time had passed, Elijah called everyone to himself. He ordered the people to soak his sacrifice three times with water. Then, Elijah said a simple prayer, and God instantly sent fire to consume the sacrifice, the altar, and the water.

In this episode we see Elijah demonstrating a great deal of confidence. He was confident enough to mock others and to set up enormous barriers for the true God. Elijah's faith was impressive. We should note, however, that when this miracle happened, Elijah turned to God in prayer; he made no pretense about his own authority. He was pointing to the power and authority of the true God. Elijah acted nobly and confidently, but God performed the miracle.

Contrast this to Jesus' miracles. When Jesus healed, he said no prayers: He did not need to turn to the Heavenly Father for His power. He spoke or touched or commanded, and people were healed. One day as Jesus entered Capernaum, a centurion asked Him to heal his servant. Jesus responded to the request by saying, "I will go and heal Him."[44] The language of the story makes it very clear that Jesus Himself had the power and authority to perform miracles. We could site many examples of Jesus' authority. He told a paralyzed man, "take up your mat and go home,"[45] He commanded the storm to "be still."[46] They were an outpouring of His personal power. These miracles were different from any of the miracles performed in the Old Testament, where the prophets made it clear that God was performing the incredible displays of His power. They were evidence that He was unique in His ministry.

Another unique facet of Christ's authority was the way He forgave sins. Jewish religious leaders often prayed for God to forgive the sins of His people. Jesus forgave sins by His own authority. Upon seeing a paralyzed man in His own town, Jesus said, "your sins are forgiven." The religious leaders of the day realized that this was not the normal procedure. In fact, they alleged that Jesus was guilty of blasphemy.[47] Pausing merely to read their thoughts, Christ went on to demonstrate His power by healing the paralyzed man. Thus, Jesus demonstrated authority not only over creation and disease, but also over sin itself.

From all this we see the uniqueness of Christ's authority. But there is more that points to Christ's uniqueness, more to show that He is the only One worth following.

Self-Centered Teaching[48]

Most people acknowledge that Jesus urged His followers to serve others, that He called His people to demonstrate self-sacrificing love. Many people fail to realize that whereas Jesus did command service and self-sacrifice, He Himself was very self-centered in His teaching; self-centered in a positive and necessary way.

Jesus' teaching focused on His mission: to live and die that others might live eternally. He alone had the power to give eternal hope and peace. Therefore, He pointed others to Himself.

Most religious leaders point us to something or someone greater than ourselves. This is true for Old Testament prophets, New Testament authors, and founders of other diverse world religions. Muhammad pointed people to Allah, and followers of Islam honor Muhammad as a great prophet but do not worship him. That is true because Muhammad pointed people away from himself. Buddha also pointed people away from himself by describing a path for living that would lead to serenity. He did not call people to worship himself.

In the book Jesus and Buddha[49] editor Marcus Borg compares quotations from Jesus and quotations from Buddha. The similarity is truly remarkable. Both call us to live morally upright lives and to love others. Both teach a kind of wisdom that changes our view of the world around us. In the introduction to this book Borg argues that the primary difference between Jesus and Buddha is that Jesus is more of a social activist than Buddha.[50] This difference between Jesus and Buddha may be true, but it is not the most significant difference between them. Buddha taught that salvation was possible by following a "path." Jesus asserted that He was the only path to salvation: "I am the way, the truth, and the life, no one comes to the Father, but by me."[51] According to Christ, moral living was not sufficient for salvation. He Himself was the center of the plan of salvation.

Jesus differed from Buddha, Muhammad, and almost all other

renowned religious leaders because He called people to Himself. The gospel of John records a number of Jesus' statements about Himself that should leave no doubt about His importance in God's plan. He called Himself the bread of life,[52] the light of the world,[53] the good shepherd,[54] and Lord.[55] He even taught that He existed before Abraham.[56] When Christ called people to follow Him, He called them to forsake family and wealth and all that was dear to them. He demanded that He be the first priority in their lives.[57]

Christ's ministry did more than introduce people to a proper way of living. He introduced people to Himself. More than a prophet who pointed people to God, He called people to Himself. If we believe Jesus to be nothing more than a good teacher, we are missing a prominent focus of His teaching. He was unique as a religious leader because He insisted that He was personally the key element in the plan of salvation.

Voluntary Suffering to Pay Our Penalty

Most of the Gospels' stories about Jesus focus on the final weeks of His life. The final days of Christ's life are central to the faith of Christians. In His dying and rising He proved Himself to be more than a mere mortal. In His death and resurrection He secured eternal salvation for all who follow Him.

One of the remarkable elements of the story of Christ's death is that He *voluntarily* suffered for us. Before going to Jerusalem for the final week of His life, Jesus explained to His disciples that He was going there with the intent of suffering and dying.[58] His suffering and death were necessary. Even though He prayed that His Father would prevent His suffering,[59] He willingly endured the torment and shame of death by crucifixion.

Christ had a number of opportunities to escape this death. He could have covertly escaped from the garden of Gethsemane before the soldiers captured Him. Peter was willing to fight in order to secure Christ's escape, but Christ rebuked him.[60] Pilate seemed to be looking for an excuse to let Jesus go free, but Jesus refused to cooperate. If Jesus had wanted to go free, He could have spoken in His own defense. He could have denied that he was the King of the Jews. His silence in the trials secured His conviction, a conviction He could have avoided.

Many religious leaders have suffered persecution, and many people have become martyrs for a cause. Jesus, though, did not merely become a martyr. A perfect man, He volunteered to die in order to secure payment for our sin. Christ's teaching was so self-centered because His voluntary sacrifice paid our penalties.

No other religion points to a just and upright God who welcomes sinners into His presence. Other religions might teach moral truths that urge people to perfection. They might also describe forgiveness as arbitrary, claiming that we never know when god will forgive us. Christians, though, trust in a God who forgives for a reason. Christ has voluntarily paid the penalties for sins.

This is one reason that it is so important to follow Christ. When we walk behind Him, we are following the One who has lived perfectly and has paid the penalty for all who follow Him. His sacrifice has satisfied God's requirements for justice.

Can you imagine a legal system that would allow a judge to arbitrarily allow some guilty people to go free, while demanding that other guilty people pay the consequences for their actions? Most would agree that such an arbitrary handling of a justice system would be a travesty. In the New Testament, however, we find rationale for God's forgiveness of sin. His forgiveness is not random; it is based on the sacrifice of His son, Jesus.

Jesus' willingness to pay the penalty for our sin is another example of the uniqueness of His ministry. It might be possible to find someone who will suffer for a righteous person, but how many innocent people would willingly suffer for someone who was guilty?

Jesus was willing to suffer because He loved us without regard for His personal well-being. He gave up His life so that we could live eternally.

Watergate and the Resurrection

The story of Jesus does not end with His death. Just as Christ's death demonstrates His love and gives us hope for forgiveness, His resurrection demonstrates His power and gives us confidence that God can do everything He said He would do.

The resurrection is a remarkable triumph. For some it is too remarkable. "How can someone who is dead and buried return to life and walk among us?" they ask. Yet this is what the Bible asserts. It is understandable that many would look at this story with a sizeable dose of skepticism. It is hardly a common occurrence for someone to return from the realm of the dead. Many want to write this off as a religious myth, like the stories of Hercules. There is a big difference, however, between the stories of Jesus and the myths of Hercules. Jesus' followers presented His stories as factual history immediately following Jesus' resurrection. They were persecuted and even put to death for telling His story. There was never such a response to Hercules.

In his book, Loving God, Charles Colson describes how the Watergate scandal during the presidency of Richard Nixon convinced him that the gospel's account of the resurrection was true.[61] You may wonder, "What does Watergate have to do with Christ's resurrection?" I asked the same question when I first heard of Colson's book. After reading it, I understood. Colson explains that various members of Richard Nixon's administration began to panic and eventually told the truth about the Watergate scandal, caving into the political and legal pressure of threatened consequences to cover up a lie. Most people refuse to suffer for a lie; when they feel pressure, they eventually tell the truth.

This tendency relates to the resurrection story; following Christ's resurrection, His followers endured a great deal of pressure, even facing incarceration or death for telling the story of His resurrection. Christ's disciples were eye witnesses of the resurrected Lord. Nowhere in history is there any record that even one of disciple confessed that the resurrection story was a deception. Not one of them offered a confession, even in the face of death, that Jesus did not actually rise from the dead. These disciples had been neither deceptive nor courageous. In fact, they had abandoned Jesus on the night He was betrayed, acting like cowards. Something marvelous must have turned them from cowards to willing sufferers for the cause of Christ.

Something marvelous had happened, of course; Jesus had risen from the dead.

Remarkably, the story of Jesus resurrection is still being told. After 2,000 years of history, millions around the world gather on Sunday mornings to celebrate the resurrection of this man. His resurrection started a movement that has outlasted any nation or political movement. His church is still witnessing to the resurrection of their Lord.

Lord, Liar, or Lunatic?[62]

In light of all that Jesus said and did, we must come to the conclusion that He was more than merely a great teacher. He was the Savior of the world. If God had offered other ways to salvation, Jesus was a lunatic for suffering unnecessarily. Moreover, if Jesus' personality and actions did not form the central part of God's salvation plan, His statements about Himself were nothing more than grandstanding, and He was a liar.

That may seem harsh, and we shudder to accuse Jesus of being a liar or a lunatic. Those who refuse to accept Him as Savior must still admit that He had a tremendous impact on the history of the world. However, if He was not God in the flesh, His words were either the overstatements of a person filled with His own ego, or they were statements made by someone who suffered from a delusional image of Himself. If either of these is true, Jesus is unworthy of being considered a great teacher. If He was a liar or a lunatic, He does not deserve the amount of attention that He has received. If, however, He was sane and did what He said He would do, He deserves nothing less than our full devotion.

The call to follow Christ is appealing because in Christ we see someone who made incredible claims about Himself, yet lived and died to serve others. In Christ, we see unparalleled self-sacrificing love combined with the power and authority to do all that we could ever ask or imagine. For this reason we cannot consider Him just another great religious leader. He is our only hope for salvation, and therefore we must follow Him.

Motorcycles and Bicycles

At the beginning of this chapter, I compared choosing a religion to shopping for a minivan. Many people believe that the difference between world religions is negligible, and that selecting a religion is nothing more than a matter of preference. In this chapter I hope that I have demonstrated the folly of that belief.

Comparing Christ to other religious leaders is not like comparing the Dodge Caravan to the Plymouth Voyager, but rather, it is like comparing a motorcycle to a bicycle. Motorcycles and bicycles share many characteristics. They each have two wheels, a seat, handlebars and brakes. Even though each of these vehicles will help you travel with more efficiency than walking, everyone knows there is a big difference between them. Motorcyclists are propelled by an engine while bicyclists have to provide the power to move.

Followers of other religions share one thing in common. In one way or another, they believe that they must live such good lives that they earn the right to enter paradise. Followers of every faith other than Christianity must earn their salvation. Their religions, like bicycles, offer teaching and guidance to help them answer life's difficult questions, and therefore assist them as they travel through life, but they do not propel them to a greater hope.

Followers of Christ do not earn their salvation. They are called to follow Christ, who has earned salvation for them. Because of His saving work, His followers are propelled by His grace to eternity in the presence of the Father. If following other religions is like riding a bicycle, following Christ is like riding a motorcycle because we do not provide the power.

As they pedal through life, followers of other religions may have a false sense of peace because of their faith. Their moral reliability may make them feel superior to others. They may credit their faith with the power to help them make decisions and find true friends. But their faith lacks the power of Christ's grace. Their bicycle may help them move through life, but it does not propel them to a greater hope for eternity.

Our power is in Christ, Who claimed a lofty position for Himself, volunteered to suffer to pay for our sins, and demonstrated His power in His resurrection.

He is worth following.

Questions for discussion/reflection:
What evidence do you see that Jesus was at least an influential leader?

Can the Bible be considered a reliable historical source for information about Jesus? Why or why not?

What kind of claims did Jesus make about Himself?

Does C.S. Lewis make a fair claim when he says that Jesus must be Lord, liar, or lunatic?

How probable is it that the disciples successfully lied about Christ's resurrection?

Chapter 4
Push Through the Pain

New life brings incredible joy.

When I first met my oldest son, the thrill of becoming a parent seemed overwhelming. I was thrilled to have a new child in our home as I experienced joy in hearing him babble and seeing him smile. I beamed with pride whenever anyone else paid attention to him. New life brought a rush of emotions that gave me strength. I endured sleepless nights with joy, laughed when he spit up on my Sunday clothes, and happily bore the extra work of caring for one more person.

Things have changed since that day.

As I write this, my oldest son is six years old. Being his father is one of my greatest joys because I love him. But the initial thrill of being a new parent has faded.

If I had believed that parenthood would be a constant state of bliss, I would have been disappointed. Parenting is a wonderful experience, but not every moment is unadulterated joy. I must confess to getting a bit grumpy when I have to wake up every hour to calm a screaming child. I no longer laugh when a baby spits up on my Sunday clothes at church, and the sound of whining voices sends a chill up my spine. I love my children, but I cannot say that every moment of parenting is pleasurable. In fact, being a parent requires hard work and great patience.

What is true when we become parents is also true when we obtain a new job, a new home, or a new vehicle. At first, the joy of newness sustains us. Eventually, though, our thrill with the newness dissipates.

Dwindling enthusiasm is also a reality in our walk with God. Initial enthusiasm does not ensure a process of unending growth in following Christ. Following Christ requires a persistent effort. We are called to pursue Him, even when the newness wears off.

The Nineteenth Mile[63]

"What am I doing?"

This question ran through Bob's mind as he tirelessly put one foot in front of the other. The marathon had started as a rather exciting event. He had spent months preparing for this race. Family members were there to support him. Adrenaline ran through his veins as he anticipated the start of the race.

As he started the race, Bob ran at a pace that was faster than he had anticipated. The excitement made running seem like a joy. But after the nineteenth mile, Bob started to experience a sense of boredom. His mind wandered as he considered picking up the pace in an attempt to qualify for the Boston Marathon. He wondered if other runners around him were becoming so fatigued that they would have to quit the race. He even thought about his nephew, who had wished him good luck at the beginning of the race. Bob had been running so long, that even though he had the strength to finish the race, he became weary of the monotony of putting one foot in front of the other.

Most runners begin a marathon with a great deal of enthusiasm. The fanfare and the thrill of the start seem to give them an extra boost of energy. However, at about the nineteenth mile, many runners start to experience fatigue. Their legs feel heavy and their lungs burn as they struggle to take in more oxygen. The thrill of the start is replaced by a monotonous routine of putting one foot in front of the other.

It is important for runners to continue running at the nineteenth mile. If they stop, they might never complete the race. But if they keep their legs moving, they will be able to struggle through three or four miles until the reality of the finish line gives them new energy to complete the race.

Following Christ can be similar to a marathon. The process begins with high levels of excitement and enthusiasm, but it does not take a long time for the fatigue and seemingly monotonous routine of the nineteenth mile infiltrates our walk with Him. The pursuit becomes less thrilling, and our endurance is tested. During those times when we feel listless in our walk with Christ, it is important that we continue to press on toward the goal that God has set before us.[64] We continue to pursue Christ with confidence that He will lead us to the glorious finish.

The Thrill that Fades

When someone first trusts Christ as her Savior, she is just beginning to realize the eternal peace of no longer carrying the burden of sin. She is a new creation in Christ.[65] Her eternal worries have just been eased. She basks in the joy of realizing that the old worries of her guilt and corruption are no longer a threat to her eternal well-being.

New life is not the only moment of feeling the thrill of following Christ. Followers of Christ will experience spiritual vitality when they see prayers answered, sense God leading them, experience an acute awareness of His peace.

I love talking to people who have recently had their eyes opened to the wonders of Christ's grace. They see things in a new light. They marvel when they see prayers answered. They are awakened to the beauty of God's creation. God's hand seems to be at work everywhere in their lives and they are quick to give Him praise for His work.

However, almost every follower of Christ will hit the nineteenth mile. The perceived routine of our daily lives can cause boredom. Our prayer lives can grow mundane, and the new life we once experienced in Christ can begin to seem like a chore.

Once we hit the nineteenth mile of following Christ, we experience a higher rate of frustrations. We might doubt the sincerity of our faith, or even question what God is doing. The nineteenth mile of following Christ can be filled with struggles and frustrations. The newness of salvation in Christ becomes a normal part of our daily lives and the initial thrill fades as the reality of sin and evil chips away at our comfort and assurance.

Like a marathon runner, when we hit the nineteenth mile of following Christ, we continue to put one foot in front of the other. We follow Christ with a single-minded focus. If we allow the worries of the world to overcome our focus on Him, we will find ourselves faltering.

Followers of Christ continue to put one foot in front of the other because they know that they are not living for the thrill of the current moment. We are living for Christ. He did not tell us that the nineteenth mile would be filled with bliss and pleasure. Rather, He taught that He was going to prepare a place for us,[66] and that we would share in the eternal delight of His Kingdom. We persevere through the trials and struggles because we have been guaranteed that the joy of the finish line will provide eternal satisfaction that will be worth the pursuit.

Jesus calls us to pursue Him so that we will know Him and experience joy. We are called to follow Christ as we experience struggles as well as when we experience the ecstatic energy of newness in Him. The disciples had the joy of following Jesus as His popularity grew because of His miracles and teaching. But they also were called to follow Jesus as He walked to the cross. Even though the disciples became confused about Christ's ministry, He called them to follow and obey.[67]

If we have had the pleasure of experiencing a "spiritual high" from walking with God, we should be grateful to Him. I believe He grants us these periods of peace to sustain us and encourage us. We need to be encouraged, because following Christ will not always bring us the experience of emotional bliss. This is why we must persevere. There will be challenges and trials as we follow Him.

Understanding Struggles

Even before sin entered the world, God called His people to perform tasks that would require effort. When God created Adam and Eve, He gave them the tasks of caring for the garden and naming the animals.[68] God assigned them the role of bearing His image to all creation, exercising His dominion and carrying out His will.[69] While these tasks may have been sheer delight in a world that was free from sin, they still required effort. Furthermore, once Adam and Eve sinned, God told Eve that He would greatly increase her pain in childbirth.[70] The wording suggests that even if sin had never entered the world, there might have been a small amount of pain or discomfort in the process of bearing children. Situations that call for effort have always been a part of God's good creation.

Many people suffer from what I call challenge aversion. They try to avoid any situation that seems challenging or difficult. Many high school graduates will not go to college because they will refuse to accept the challenge of studying. Many people will not submit an application for a job interview because they fear rejection. Our fears often paralyze us and keep us from facing challenges.

As we follow Christ, we will face challenges, struggles, and hardships. Jesus told His disciples that the world would hate His followers.[71] If Christians cling to the belief that they will never have to face challenges or struggles, they will be disappointed. For this reason, the New Testament calls Christ's followers to persevere through trials and hardships.[72] Let us consider the nature of the struggles that Christians will face.

1. Struggles due to our own guilt. Sometimes we face trials and hardships because we are guilty. When we have made mistakes or sinned, we often have to pay a price. We take great comfort in knowing that Christ has paid the ultimate price for our sins, but sometimes, though, sinful actions affect our lives. If I make a habit of telling lies, I may have to endure the consequence of lost trust. If I rob a bank, I might be sentenced to spend time in prison.

These effects of sin are consistent with God's forgiveness. Once we are forgiven, God takes away the ultimate consequence of our sin, eternity apart from Him. However, the damage that sin does in this world can still come back to haunt us. Sin creates struggles and hardships even for followers of Christ who have been forgiven.

Sometimes, however, we suffer simply because we make poor judgments. I might make a foolish decision to go ice fishing on a warm winter day, only to fall through the ice and suffer. I might invest in a company that promises outstanding growth, only to see that company declare bankruptcy. Even though such actions are not sinful, they demonstrate a direct relationship to our decisions and their consequences. Most of us will instinctively understand that we are responsible for a great deal of the struggles we experience in our lives, but personal foolishness and rebellion does not explain all of our struggles.

2. Struggles due to evil in our world. I once visited a man who had just been diagnosed with cancer. His first comment for me was, "I can't help wondering which one of my sins caused this. I must have done something terrible." This man is not alone in his fears. Many people make the mistake of believing that every struggle they face is a result of their sin or poor decisions.

The idea that we cause every bad thing that happens in our lives is not new. In the gospel of John, Christ and His disciples met a man who had been born blind. The disciples asked Jesus why this man was blind, wonder whether he had committed some gross sin, or if his parents had been guilty. Jesus corrected their thinking by explaining that neither he nor his parents caused his blindness.[73]

Though he walked faithfully with God, the Old Testament saint, Job, suffered a variety of afflictions. After he lost his health, wealth, and family to what seemed a tragic turn of events, his friends came to counsel him. They insisted in their talks that Job must have angered God in some way, and that he should repent. Near the end of the book of Job we find that Job's friends were wrong in their assessment.[74] Both they and Job were unable to see that Satan was wreaking havoc in Job's life, even though Job walked with God.

Often, we encounter sad events that we have done nothing to cause. When Adam and Eve first sinned, they unleashed a wave of evil that still wreaks havoc in this world today. Bad things often injure good people for no clear reason. Car accidents harm innocent people, criminals victimize others, and young children contract terrible illnesses. We cannot reasonably blame people who suffer such afflictions. People will often suffer in their lives even though they are innocent.

The Psalms give us insightful examples of prayer in times of affliction. For example, in Psalm 13, David pleads with God to show him mercy, because he is innocently suffering at the hands of his enemies. David's prayer makes it clear that he has done nothing wrong to cause his enemies to treat him badly. He bases his prayer on the promise of Psalm 1, where the Bible teaches that those who are faithful to God will prosper.[75] In the process of praying, David reaffirms his faith, despite the circumstance, and rejoices in God's salvation. David comes to understand that even though he is experiencing struggles, he will be rescued by God. The Bible does not promise freedom from every kind of suffering. Followers of Christ will suffer. The good news is that the one we follow will one day take all of our suffering away, and He will make everything right.

3. Struggles to improve. We endure yet another kind of suffering or struggle: the struggle to improve. There are struggles in our lives that are not necessarily evil. In fact, they are usually for our benefit.

When my son Luke was six years old, he decided that he wanted to learn how to ride a bike without training wheels. We took the training wheels off of his bike, and for more than a week, he struggled. He started to believe he would never be able to ride a "two-wheeler," and he worried about falling and getting hurt. He realized that he had to attain good balance, the ability to steer, and the ability to start and stop. There were instances he even suffered minor injuries when he fell to the ground.

No sin caused Luke's struggle. He did not fall because he was guilty. He was falling as a result of his effort to acquire a new skill. Even if he had suffered a more serious injury, no one would conclude that his wounds were a result of guilt and rebellion. He could have skinned his knees, suffered bruises, or even broken bones. This would not have been the result of evil, however; it would have been the natural result of struggling to become better.

There is a price to pay for every effort we make to improve ourselves. Athletes suffer the pain of intense conditioning. Entrepreneurs work long hours and often lose money as they strive to start their own businesses. Children in kindergarten must struggle to master concepts surrounding letters and numbers. We encourage people to face these struggles because there is something worthwhile for those who endure.

The same principle is true for followers of Christ. Life's most worthwhile endeavor is to follow Jesus, for in Him we find our only enduring comfort and peace. Our pursuit of Jesus requires us to reach beyond ourselves as we focus on Him. Inevitably, that will produce a struggle.

When we begin our pursuit of Christ, we experience a thrill. At first God may seem very near. It may seem as though He answers every prayer directly.[76] As we grow, however, we may experience times of spiritual lethargy. What can be called spiritual lethargy occurs for a number of reasons. For example, sin that lingers in our lives can hinder our walk with God, or the evil in this world can stunt our spiritual growth. If we allow our lethargy to smother our pursuit of Christ, spiritual growth will be stunted. If, however, we continue putting one foot in front of the other and pursue Christ, even though it becomes difficult, sooner or later, we will again experience the joy and peace that typified the beginning of our walk with Him.

We can expect struggles in our walk with God as we go through the process of maturing in faith. The good news is that God can use all of these struggles for our benefit. This is why we are told to rejoice in all kinds of trying circumstances.[77] God can make our circumstances useful for His purposes.

This does not mean, however, that God desires all kinds of struggles in our lives. He is not the author and inventor of evil. He did not desire that Adam and Eve sin and unleash a wave of sin and evil in our world, but He is powerful and loving enough to manipulate the evil in our world and to use it for His purposes. Most likely, we are unable to see what God is doing in the times when we feel that He is far away. In those moments He might be preparing us for a wonderful part of His plan. We must be careful that we do not fall prey to the notion that every moment spent following Christ will be one of spiritual ecstasy. His yoke may be easy and His burden may be light,[78] but there is still a yoke and a burden for His followers.

We follow One who will see us through our struggles. We persevere through trials in the confidence that He walks with us.

The Direction of Our Hearts

Looking to Christ gives a focus and direction for our lives, and helps us avoid pitfalls as we struggle to follow Him.

I always have a difficult time motivating myself to mow our lawn, probably because I have a terrible time making the first pass through it. The first pass is the most important because if you set a nice straight path, the rest of the lawn comes out in a straight pattern. If you deviate from a straight line, however, the entire lawn ends up with crooked paths that will remain until the next time you mow. I used to mow in crooked paths, because I could never mow a straight first pass. One day, though, my neighbor gave me some advice that I will never forget. He told me that I was mowing crooked because I was focusing on the wrong thing. As I began mowing, I was so intent on my path that I would inevitably veer from side to side. He advised me to focus instead a fixed object beyond my yard, perhaps on a neighbor's tree. He explained that if I walked toward a fixed object as I mowed the first pass, my path would be straight. I skeptically tried his advice but was pleasantly surprised to find that my paths were straight when I focused on a fixed object beyond my yard.

Jesus' call to follow Him makes it clear that He should be the fixed object of our constant focus. We can avoid common obstacles and deviations of life when we follow Him. Too often we err in our walk because we become distracted by daily problems. These distractions cause us to deviate from our path of following Christ. The Bible gives us a solution to this problem when it says that when we focus our attention on God and place our trust in Him, He works to straighten our paths.[79]

The Bible is filled with instances of God issuing orders that required His people to pay attention to Him. "Follow Me" was Christ's repeated call.[80] He also issued a similar command: "Come to Me."[81] The Old Testament repeatedly makes it clear that the Lord wanted His people to walk with Him.[82] As we notice the repetition of these phrases, it becomes apparent that God desires that our hearts be directed to obey Him. Jesus taught that the greatest commandment was to love God "with all your heart and with all your soul and with all your mind."[83] This kind of devotion requires a resolute effort to pursue our Lord. It demands that we set our sights on Him as we follow.

Maintaining Our Focus

Keeping our hearts focused on Christ in times of trouble is a difficult challenge for Christians. It is very easy for us to become overwhelmed by difficult circumstances and to forget, even for a short time, that Christ is in control. When we do this, our walk with Christ suffers.

The gospel of Matthew tells a story about Peter walking on water.[84] He demonstrated a great deal of faith in merely asking Christ if he could get out of the boat and walk.[85] Not only did he demonstrate a bold confidence in Christ by asking for permission to walk on water, he also followed through and obeyed when Christ told Him to come. His response is a model for the way in which Christ's followers should respond to Him. The thrill of walking did not last, though, for the storms started, and diverted Peter's focus. Instead of looking to Christ, he became concerned about the wind and the waves. He looked away from Christ and started to sink.

As a fallible human, I can hardly blame Peter for looking away. I doubt that I would even have asked for permission to walk on water. If I had been placed in that situation, I would have lost my focus on my Savior and embraced the temptation to look away. When we hear a noise, our natural reflex is to look.

Peter's distraction caused him to lose his solid footing, and he immediately began to sink. In that frightening moment, Peter had the presence of mind to look back to Jesus and ask for salvation. Jesus rescued him, and they returned to the boat. Jesus' words to Peter following this experience astonish me. He tells Peter that he has little faith and asks why he doubted.

Little faith?

From my perspective, Peter demonstrated tremendous faith: he asked to walk on water. Moreover, he obeyed his Lord by stepping out of the boat. The only mistake he seemed to make was reacting to the storm by turning his head.

But the turning of the head is enough to damage our walk with God. His followers are called to constantly focus on Him. We are called to pray continuously.[86] There are many dangers that exist. There are many things that will seek to pull our attention away from Christ. When we lose our focus on Him, even briefly, our walk suffers. The fears of life can overwhelm. The insatiable nature of our human desire can eat away at our spiritual growth. When we allow room for anything else to sit on the throne of our hearts, we are not focused on following Christ.

Sometimes people make a conscious decision to reject Christ. They might believe that God does not have their best interest at heart, or that He is not good enough or powerful enough to help. They intentionally make a decision to turn away from Christ and follow another path. In my experience, however, this is not the usual way people go astray. It seems far more common that people lose sight of Christ because they become distracted. Their focus is compromised. They fall prey to "spiritual amnesia."[87] They forget to look to God. These distractions are not the results of evil intentions or rebellious inclinations; they are a result of a heart whose focus has been altered.

The people of Israel suffered from this amnesia in the Old Testament. The book of Judges is a series of stories that follow the same pattern. First, God's people begin to forget what God has done for them. Second, as a result of turning from Him they begin to suffer. Third, they see their condition and turn back to God. Finally, God hears their cries and sends a leader to free them from their troubles.

The book of Judges does not draw a picture of a nation that intentionally turns from God. It seems as though they become thoughtless: they forget to turn to Him, and they go astray. Like Peter, they were not trying to rebel against God; other things simply drew their attention away from Him. As a result of this distraction, God's people were pulled into an evil way of living that resulted in their separation from God. Seemingly innocent distractions can have catastrophic implications.

Jesus' response to Peter was a matter-of-fact statement. It is a fact that all of us have very little faith. We are all easily distracted. Our attention to Christ wavers as we experience the ebb and flow of following Him through triumphs and trials. Thankfully, we need only faith the size of a mustard seed for God to use us in powerful ways.[88] The story of Peter walking on water should serve as a challenge for followers of Christ to intensify our focus on Him. We should practice looking to Him and pursuing Him in all that we do.

The Paradoxical Pursuit

Following Christ after His ascension into heaven puts us in a situation that seems impossible. On one hand, we are called to pursue our Lord with all of our heart, soul, mind, and strength.[89] On the other hand, we are called to pursue someone who remains physically unseen.[90] How can we follow someone we cannot see?

When Peter walked on water, he had the benefit of seeing the physical presence of Jesus. He could have literally focused his eyes upon the person of Jesus. We do not have that option today. We walk by faith, not by sight.[91] When we speak of turning our eyes toward Jesus, we are speaking figuratively. We are to see Him with the eyes of faith; eyes that are able to trust He guides and cares for us, despite His physical absence. Even though following someone who remains unseen seems impossible, faith makes it possible.

Our ability to follow an unseen God can be enhanced when we begin to notice what can be seen. We can see that God is at work. He causes the world to rotate around the sun, brings the sunshine and the rain that cause crops to grow, gives life to new-born babies, and transforms hardened hearts to be attuned to His leading. We can follow Christ with the eyes of faith because we see evidence around us that God is at work.

However, even though we see evidence of God's work, walking by faith will present two unique challenges. First, we are skeptical people, and we must learn to trust someone who is unseen. Second, we are easily distracted. Like Peter, our attention can be drawn away from Christ by circumstances around us. In our situation, however, this becomes an especially dangerous trap, because we have the difficult task of focusing on someone who is not physically present.

In order to faithfully follow someone who is unseen, we would be wise to develop spiritual disciplines. The word discipline is closely related to the word disciple. This is not a coincidence. To be a disciple (or a follower) means that we try to develop patterns that cause us to resemble the One we follow. While disciplines may initially appear to constrict our freedom, they actually liberate us from our natural inclinations to walk away from God.

The Role of Spiritual Disciplines

Spiritual disciplines liberate us to follow Christ by causing us to grow in our assurance that God will be faithful. As we practice spiritual disciplines, we are better able to trust that God will be reliable and that He will continue to guide.

When I was in first grade, my family moved into a new house. One of my personal struggles associated with that move was trying to walk to the bathroom at night. Since I did not want to turn on lights and wake up my family, I had to wander without the use of my sight. At first, every journey to the bathroom was filled with bumping into walls and tripping over furniture. As the months passed, I became much more proficient at walking to the bathroom in the dark. The more I made the journey, the more I learned the landscape of our new home. I even developed the ability to make that trip without sticking out my arms to grope in the dark. I was able to make the journey with greater ease because repetition engrained the proper steps in my mind. I learned the locations of the walls and furniture, and I learned to trust that I could navigate around the obstacles. The repetition made the journey much easier.

Spiritual disciplines help develop the reassurance that God is always faithful. As we focus the eyes of faith upon Him, we learn through repetition and experience that He is faithful,[92] that He will not forsake us,[93] and that He will make our paths straight.[94]

Spiritual disciplines are a further blessing to us because they cause us to focus our attention on Christ. As we repeat the habits of looking to Christ, our new habits become a second nature. God begins to transform us so that we automatically turn our focus to following Christ and doing His will.

Pursuing Christ should be an intentional process. If we are not actively seeking Him, we can easily lose our focus and go astray. Pursuing Christ means that we will incorporate disciplines into the routines of our lives.

Christians have practiced a variety of spiritual disciplines that cause them to turn their attention toward Christ.[95] The traditional spiritual disciplines include praying, scripture reading, meditating, fasting, living simply, serving, confessing, simplicity, service, confession, and worshipping.[96] Many Christians have written about developing these habits to enhance their walk with God.[97]

If you are a follower of Christ, I encourage you to develop disciplines that help you focus on Him. Perhaps you are already practicing some of these disciplines. Worshipping with others weekly, praying before meal times, and reading scripture or devotional material regularly are just some of the disciplines that many practice. You might do this without even realizing that such practices can be called spiritual disciplines.

As you develop spiritual disciplines, keep in mind that their purpose is to focus our attention on God. Do not allow your spiritual disciplines to become a matter of pride. If you are proud of the frequency and eloquence of your prayers, you have turned your attention from God to your own abilities.

Spiritual disciplines can help us focus on God, but they do not propel us forward in our walk with Him. Our habits and disciplines will help us keep in step with His plan for our lives, but Jesus is responsible for advancing His plans. He is the author and perfecter of our faith,[98] so we should take care to avoid the trap of becoming proud of our disciplines. Our disciplines are merely practices that help us fix our eyes on Him.

Spiritual disciplines are like a sail on a boat.[99] The sail does not move the boat. Instead, the sail helps the boat take full advantage of the wind. Our spiritual disciplines do not make us righteous. They help us focus on Christ so that we are better able to be moved by the Holy Spirit.

The Obstacle of Focusing on the Plan

As we mature in our walk with God, we will grow in our desire to follow God's plans for our lives. I will regularly pray that God will provide opportunities for me to serve Him. I will ask for wisdom to know His will. I will pray for courage to obey Him.

As I pray for wisdom and guidance, I find myself attempting to discern God's will for my future. This is quite normal. College students pray for wisdom as they choose a degree for their future careers. They try to imagine how God will use them and follow His plans accordingly.

However, there is a danger in anticipating God's plan. Even when we try to discern God's leading, we can lose sight of Christ as we focus on "the plan." I have made the mistake of feeling certain that I knew God's plan, and then following my own instincts. If I believed God wanted me to witness to a friend, I would force myself upon that friend and speak the truth, never pausing to consider how God would have me witness to that friend. If I believed God wanted me to offer help to an acquaintance, I would quickly decide how I wanted to offer help, rather than devoting myself to discern how God would have me help. When I have done this, I have been guilty of forgetting to walk with God. I have attempted to anticipate God's leading and run ahead of Him. Even if I was correct in discerning His will, I had to learn that I must seek His guidance as I strive to live for Him.

I grew up in the town of DeMotte, Indiana, and I currently live in Grand Rapids, Michigan. DeMotte is a small town in the northwest corner of Indiana. If I were giving someone directions to get from Grand Rapids to DeMotte, I would tell him to follow the road signs to Chicago for the first two hours of the trip. Shortly after crossing the Indiana border, the driver would need to quit following the signs to Chicago, and follow a new set of directions.

Some travelers might become upset once they left the path to Chicago. They might have become so set on the goal of moving towards Chicago, that they feel cheated once the directions change. Some travelers might even accuse me of misleading them once I told them to quit following the road signs to Chicago.

My directions to DeMotte were never intended to get people to Chicago. However, some might misread my directions. As they follow the plan, they anticipate the wrong destination.

You might think it would be silly for someone to become angry or frustrated with me as they followed my directions to DeMotte. People should know that a trip to DeMotte will not end up in Chicago. Travelers should realize that sooner or later the road signs to Chicago would differ from the directions to a small town in Indiana.

Those who are following Christ, however, often make the mistake of trying to anticipate where God is leading them. They come to God in prayer, asking for His guidance. They might believe He is leading them to open a business, become a missionary, or marry their high school sweetheart. As they make decisions that bring them closer to realizing their anticipated plans, they begin to experience difficulties. Often, they are disappointed when their original hopes are not realized. As they face disappointment many will be tempted to blame God for misleading them, believing that He intentionally set them up for failure. They believed He revealed His will clearly to them, by mystically revealing His will. Once their plans are altered, and they begin to pursue new goals for their lives, they feel somewhat bewildered and lost.

Following Christ can be like taking a trip from Grand Rapids, Michigan to DeMotte, Indiana. We may listen to Christ's instructions and have a sense that we know where He is leading, but might be disappointed to find out that we made a mistake in trying to anticipate the final destiny. We are also prone to make mistakes when we try to anticipate what God is going to do in the near future or when we focus on our idea of "God's plan" for our lives, rather than turning to God for constant guidance and direction. God does not mislead us. Foolishly, we often try to run ahead of Him when we think we know the plan.

Remember, if you are a follower of Christ, God has secured your final destination. He does not tell us ahead of time exactly what will happen before we get there. Be assured that He will take you to be with Him in His Kingdom one day. In the meantime, do not try to anticipate

His immediate plans; focus on Him.

Following through Setbacks

Another struggle that followers of Christ will face is the disappointment of apparent failure. Consider Moses' life. God spoke clearly to Moses from a burning bush.[100] Despite Moses' hesitation, God insisted that he go to rally the people of Israel to prepare them for freedom, and to stand before Pharaoh and demand the release of God's people. From our perspective, we see that God was in charge of this entire process, for He eventually parted the waters of the Red Sea to free His people. Yet between the burning bush and Red Sea, Moses experienced at least ten failures as he attempted to convince Pharaoh to release Israel. Ten failures! That is more than enough to make most people wonder if God is really going to do what He promised. Many would quit trying to follow God. But even though Moses experienced temporary setbacks, he continued to follow God's leading. Eventually, God freed His people and Moses' failures proved to be insignificant.

We will have times of feeling as though we are between the burning bush and the Red Sea. We have sought God's will, and we are confident that He has been guiding us, yet we still experience setbacks and failures.

I know a pastor whose church started an outreach ministry in its neighborhood. At the beginning of the process the leaders sought God's face and felt God's hand guiding them as key people became leaders for the new ministry. There was a great deal of excitement in the community and in the church. Many believed God was doing something wonderful. Only five years later, all four of those key leaders had left that ministry. What was God doing? Did this pastor and other leaders misunderstand God's leading? Not necessarily. In our weakness, we cannot fathom what God is doing through our setbacks and failures. In His time, God brought Israel out of Egypt, even though it seemed like the failures would just keep adding up. For this church, there were struggles and questions, but God provided new leadership to continue the work He began.

As people living between the burning bush and the Red Sea, we must persevere as we focus on Christ and pursue Him. Perseverance is necessary as we grow past the initial thrill of following Christ and begin to face the struggles and setbacks that are common for followers of Christ.

Questions for discussion/reflection:

When have you experienced hitting the nineteenth mile? In your vocation? In your personal life? In your spiritual life? How did you respond?

What's the difference between suffering as a consequence of your own sin and struggling even though you are innocent?

Do you think it is common for Christians to experience a letdown after going through a time of spiritual ecstasy?

What are some common spiritual disciplines that you practice? Which spiritual disciplines do you think you should work to incorporated into your routine?

How can spiritual disciplines keep us from falling into "spiritual amnesia"?

Chapter 5
Peak Performance Requires Total Commitment

I am probably not completely useless when it comes to mechanical repairs and home improvement projects; I know how to change a light bulb, and I can tighten a loose screw. But if a project requires any kind of skill, I call Mike Ross, a home-remodeler in western Michigan. I like calling Mike, because our relationship is very clearly defined. I tell him what I would like to see changed in my home, and he does it. After the job is done, I pay the bill, and I probably will not see Mike again until the next time I have a home improvement project. Mike and I are both satisfied with this kind of working relationship. The expectations are clear, yet not overly intrusive into each other's lives. We each leave the projects satisfied.

You might be tempted to think that Mike and I do not like each other, but this is not true. I think Mike is a warm and friendly person. I have discovered that he is a man of integrity, and I admire him. I greatly appreciate him and the work he has done for me. I would like to think that the admiration is mutual. However, I do not believe either one of us expects to develop a deep intimacy in our friendship. We are satisfied with the limited contact we have.

Many people want their relationship with Christ to look like my relationship with Mike Ross. They want the convenience of turning to Christ in prayer whenever they have a project for Him. They are willing to negotiate to get what they want, but they hope that Christ will not ask too much of them. They would like Christ to answer their requests, offer Him a prayer of thanks, and part ways until the next time they have an urgent need.

Most people do not dislike Christ; they just do not desire a deep intimacy with Him. They are satisfied with the limited contact that comes when they turn to Christ in times of need, and they hope Christ will always be available to satisfy their requests.

Christ is not satisfied with half-hearted attempts to appease Him when it conveniently fits our schedules. Even though Mike Ross and I might be mutually satisfied with our working relationship, Christ demands more. He calls us to be completely devoted to Him. His love demands a high level of commitment from His followers.

The call to follow Christ is not a call to be taken lightly. Jesus' intent is not to satisfy our whims and fulfill all of our desires in exchange for occasional prayers or half-hearted attempts to obey His commands. His intent is to bring us back into a right relationship with God, to give us salvation. He calls us to respond with complete commitment to Him.

Not an Entertainer

Throughout His ministry, Christ performed many miracles that demanded attention such as healing the sick, providing food for large crowds, calming storms, walking on water, and even raising a man from the dead. These miracles were signs that He was from God. His ministry and teaching were authentic. The crowds responded to Him favorably because of His miracles.

However, Jesus did not perform these miracles for sheer entertainment. Before His death, Jesus was brought before Herod,[101] whose duty was to determine whether Jesus was guilty of rebellion against the civil authorities. The Bible tells us that Herod was pleased to see Jesus because He wanted to see some of the handiwork of this famous miracle man. Jesus' response to Herod is surprising. He neither answered Herod's questions, nor did He perform a miracle. He simply stood trial in complete silence. This seemed to be a golden opportunity! Jesus had the attention of rulers and authority figures. He could have demonstrated definitively that He was God in the flesh. But instead he was silent.

From a human perspective it seems as though Jesus missed a golden opportunity. He could have made a powerful impression on Herod and other officials. But the goal of Jesus' ministry was not merely to impress people and leave them with good memories. He came to change the condition of their lives and give them an opportunity to stand in the presence of God.

Many people approach Jesus with the attitude of Herod. They are glad to see Him because He might be able to help them or because they enjoy His stories. After all, some of the stories He told are the best-known stories in the world. The parables of the prodigal son[102] and the Good Samaritan[103] are still read and widely known, even outside of Christian circles. Some may turn to Jesus for help with a difficult situation. People struggling in their marriages may turn to Jesus. People who are having a debate may want to quote Jesus in order to strengthen their argument; and people who are ill may pray to Jesus for His healing touch.

Please do not misunderstand me. There is nothing wrong with turning to Jesus to ask for His help. We need His help. However, if we turn to Jesus only when we think He can immediately assist us, we are not being faithful to the call to follow Him. Jesus asks more from His followers than attention when it is convenient. He asks for a commitment.

Our commitment to Christ is a blessing to us. I cannot think of anything in this world that brings lasting joy without a commitment. Absent parents miss out on many joys of rearing children and developing a deep and lasting relationship with them. A father who shows up only when it is convenient may have some good memories of his child, but the parent-child bond will be less than it should be. The reverse is true, too. A grown daughter who pays attention to her mother only when she needs something may indeed have all of her requests fulfilled, but she will still be missing something. She misses the opportunity to develop an intimate relationship with her mom. Deep, meaningful relationships only happen when we make a commitment to nourish them.

Our relationship with Christ is similar. If we pray only when we need a favor, or look at His word only when we need an answer to a question, we are missing numerous opportunities to develop an intimate relationship with God. In order to develop intimacy with God, we must devote ourselves to following Him.

The Cost of Following

The idea that following Christ will be costly became clear to me as I learned about the life of a man who was willing to give his life in order to follow Christ.

Dietrich Bonhoeffer was a pastor in Germany during the time Hitler came to power. Because he refused to remain silent as he saw the Nazis rise to power, Bonhoeffer paid a tremendous price by spending time in a Nazi concentration during World War II. There he became a pastor to other prisoners as they suffered together at the hands of evil. Before the war was over, the Nazis murdered him. Bonhoeffer understood that following Christ can be very difficult. This becomes clear in his book, The Cost of Discipleship,[104] in which he argues convincingly that following Christ is a costly pursuit. Bonhoeffer's pursuit of Christ eventually cost him his life.

One of the most memorable phrases from Bonhoeffer's book is "grace is not cheap."[105] It is a gift of God, free to all who follow Christ, but Christ paid for that grace with His life. Bonhoefer argues that receiving this gift of God may require Christ's followers to lose their lives. Jesus said, "Whoever finds his life will lose it, and whoever loses his life for my sake will find it."[106] Following Christ requires that I lose myself in Him. I must give up the things of this world that are important to me, I must practice self denial,[107] and I must be willing to abandon my family[108] and all I own[109] to follow Him.

I need to hear Bonhoeffer's call to self-sacrificing discipleship. I can fall prey to the lie that life should always be easy. Bonhoeffer's words are a stinging indictment to people who have grown accustomed to on-demand service and quick solutions to trivial problems. The culture of quick-fixes and easy solutions has infiltrated our faith. Too many people, who call themselves Christians, only follow Christ when they find it convenient. They like the idea of calling Christ their Savior, but cringe at the idea of calling Him their Lord. A savior is someone is willing and able to rescue you. The title, lord, on the other hand, indicates authority. Jesus is both Savior and Lord. As our Lord, He has the right to demand our lives for His glory.

Convenient Relationships

We often develop friendships around surprisingly arbitrary circumstances. Our friends are usually our classmate in school, our next-door neighbors, or our fellow workers. Many of our deep friendships are very warm, deep, and lasting, but they seem to happen almost by chance.

Some of my dearest friends were classmates in high school and college. Dan and I were classmates from kindergarten through our senior year in high school, and lived less than one mile apart. We attended the same church, took similar courses in school, and played on our school's basketball team.

Dave and I met at Calvin College. We were roommates for two years. We formed a friendship around watching basketball games and playing cards. We did not go out of our way to meet each other. Our common school experiences brought us together.

If I had been two years younger or older, I probably would never have become friends with Dave or Dan. There are many factors that were at work to allow our friendship to grow, factors over which I had no control.

To some degree, my friendships with Dan and Dave resulted from convenience. We were in the same school, shared the same classes and teachers, studied together and spent weekend evenings together, enjoyed common activities, and even attended the same churches. Many common, convenient factors brought us together.

I still treasure my friendships with Dave and Dan. Some of my fondest memories include them. They had a tremendous influence in my life. Although I don't see them nor talk to them very often, there is a comfortable feeling between us that I hope will never fade.

Despite this comfortable feeling, I cannot say that I am still close to them, at least not the way that I once was. Years and distance have separated us. We live in different states or on different continents. I once was able to tell you the secrets in their lives; at one time they knew my daily routine as well as I did. Today, however, we do not know each other all that well. I forget if Dan has four or five children; and I am almost certain that I couldn't tell you their names. I haven't seen Dave for over a year, and I could not tell you what his plans look like for the next couple of months.

For relationships to endure there needs to be a commitment that goes beyond convenient circumstances. When I married my wife, I made a promise to stay with her as long as we both shall live. Even though we met under the convenient circumstance of attending the same college, we have made a commitment to be together. Since we desire to have a lasting intimacy between us, we will not rely on convenient circumstances to help our relationship flourish.

Intimacy with Christ

Christ wants us to experience an enduring intimacy with Him, and therefore, He is not satisfied when we rely on convenient circumstances to strengthen our relationship with Him. He does not want us to admire Him from a distance with a warm fondness. He wants ongoing, regular contact with us. He gave His life for us, and He asks for us to submit our lives completely to Him.

Perhaps the word "intimacy" makes you a little uneasy. It is one of those "touchy-feely" words that make you squeamish. Maybe you believe that intimacy has a sexual connotation, and therefore it is unfitting to use that word to describe our relationship with God.

I admit that the word intimacy has its drawbacks. However, I cannot think of a better word to describe the kind of relationship God wants with His people. Fondness does not capture the quality that describes a proper relationship with God. God wants us to be fond of Him, but we can be fond of someone without ever seeing them or talking to them. Closeness is problematic too. We can be physically close to people (like neighbors or co-workers) without having any personal interactions. Friendly is insufficient because we can be friendly or polite towards people without even knowing their names.

Intimacy indicates a deep level of interpersonal knowledge. It is the quality that Christ prayed for when He said to His Father, "I pray for those who will believe in me...that all of them may be one, Father, just as you are in me and I am in you. May they also be in us so that the world may believe that you have sent me. I have given them the glory that you gave me, that they may be one as we are one: I in them and you in me."[110]

Christ wants us to experience intimate unity with Him. He desires the kind of intimacy in a good marriage, when a husband and a wife know each others thoughts and desires. Best friends often have this quality in their friendship. Long-time teammates on a sports team will demonstrate this kind of unity when they know each others thoughts and movements without speaking. Christ wants us to experience that kind of single-mindedness with Him. But it does not happen by accident. Intimacy with Christ is only developed when we dedicate ourselves to faithfully following Him.

Jesus will not tolerate a commitment that fades because it is inconvenient. He demands our attention. He calls His followers to cast aside whatever would distract them from following Him. For some of us, this may mean that we should turn our backs on things that interest us. We may need to forsake busyness so that we do not forsake Him.[111]

Practitioners of Faith

I participated in a number of sports when I was younger. In high school I particularly enjoyed playing on the basketball team. I enjoyed the competition of the games, the camaraderie among my teammates, and even the practices. Participating in that sport taught me much about cooperation and self-discipline. I learned the value of accepting losses with grace and taking orders from people in authority. I like to think that I gained many valuable lessons from participating in sports.

Today, I still like basketball. My love and appreciation for the game has made me a fan. Every March I have to clear my schedule as much as possible so that I can watch the NCAA basketball tournament. During the NBA finals, my wife must gently remind me that I do not need to see every single game.

In a deep part of my psyche, I still want to call myself a basketball player. In good conscience, however, I cannot. It has been over fifteen years since I have participated in a practice or played in an organized game. I have not even played a pick-up game for over three years. The closest I get to actually playing in my current phase of life is when I attempt to lift my four-year-old son, Isaac, so that he can put the ball through the hoop in our driveway. In short, I am no longer a player, but merely a spectator.

Following Christ is not a spectator sport. We do not participate in Christ's plan for His Kingdom plans merely by admiring His work from a distance. We are called to obedient action; to put or faith into practice.

I heard a caller on a radio talk show who identified herself as a "non-practicing Catholic." This description struck me as odd. How can one be a "non-practicing" member of a religious group? The description seemed to me like someone saying, "I am a basketball player who doesn't play basketball." I understand what this caller meant. She was trying to say that she believed the teachings of the Catholic Church were true, but that she did not put those teachings into action.

Jesus does not acknowledge the category of "non-practicing" followers. He is very clear that the call to follow Him is a call to obedient action. Jesus frequently reminded His disciples that they had to act on His words.

If you love me you will obey what I command.[112]

Teach them to obey everything I have commanded you.[113]

Blessed are those…who hear the word of God and obey it.[114]

You are my friends if you do what I command.[115]

James goes even further in describing the importance of practicing what we believe.

Do not merely listen to the word, and so deceive yourselves. Do what it says. Anyone who listens to the word but does not do what it says is like a man who looks at his face in a mirror and, after looking at himself, goes away and immediately forgets what he looks like. But the man who looks intently into the perfect law that gives freedom, and continues to do this, not forgetting what he has heard, but doing it—he will be blessed in what he does.[116]

True followers of Christ are practitioners of their faith. Despite their flaws and lapses in judgment, they participate in Christ's plans by acting on His words. Following Christ is not a spectator sport. It is a life of acting in obedience to His commands.

Minimizing Commitment

At times I have made the mistake of minimizing my commitment to Christ. I have tried to figure out the least I need to do in order to pacify God's anger against me. As I have studied God's word and talked with other believers, I have witnessed a number of ways that Christ's followers minimize their response to Christ's grace. In the following paragraphs, I will help you understand what I mean. We will consider four words that are used among Christians to describe how we should respond to God: repent, faith, worship, and tithe. We will see that many of us will abuse these concepts by seeing them as simple obligations, rather than as guides to draw us into a more intimate walk with Christ.

Repent. Repent means to turn. When John the Baptist cried out for people to repent,[117] he was telling them to turn away from an old way of life and turn to a new way. On one occasion in Christ's ministry, the Jewish leaders brought to Him a woman who was guilty of adultery. Most people who have heard the story will remember that Jesus responded with grace to the sin of this woman. The part of the story that we might forget is Jesus command to the woman, "Leave your life of sin."[118] This was a call to repentance. Jesus was willing to forgive, but He also called this woman to leave her old ways and to begin a new life.

If we minimize the call of Christ, we reduce repentance to remorse or confession. Confession is an acknowledgment of guilt; remorse is a feeling of guilt. Both are common in a person who is truly repentant, but neither is the same as repentance. Jesus did not ask the woman if she felt bad about her sin; He did not even ask her to confess her sin. He simply told her to leave that way of living.

Many Christians hold the false idea that following Christ is nothing more than sinning today so that they can ask for forgiveness tomorrow. They believe that Christianity is like a "get out of jail free" card. Certainly, Jesus is willing to forgive, but He also calls believers to turn from the old paths of sin and follow Him.

Faith. Faith is a wholehearted response to Christ. It encompasses our thoughts, emotions, and actions. If we think that faith can be reduced to an intellectual acknowledgment of scriptural teaching, then we are minimizing the call to follow Christ. Followers of Christ are not only called to have faith, but to be faithful. When we think of having faith, we think of believing certain statements to be true. Being faithful means that what we believe has implication for how we live.

In the field of psychology, there are three well-known schools of counseling: affective, behavioral, and cognitive. Affective psychologists focus their attention on how a person feels. Behavioral psychologists counsel patients and help them develop tools to change their behaviors. Cognitive psychologists attempt to help their clients think differently about their lives. Psychologists understand that the psyche of a person includes thoughts, emotions, and behaviors. True faith affects each of these areas of our lives. It involves knowledge (thought) of who God is and what He has done for us. It gives us an assurance (emotion) that Christ's mercy is extended to us. It works to transform you so that we live differently (behavior).

Worship. During most of my childhood years, I believed worship was an obligation that could be satisfied by ceremonial acts of devotion. I assumed that I had fulfilled my duty to worship if I prayed before meals, participated in daily family devotions, and attended church on Sunday. If I were to say an extra prayer at some point during the week, I believed I had attained some "extra credit" for my worship obligation. Today, I suspect that many Christians think of worship similarly, but the Bible has a broader view of worship in the life of a follower of Christ.

Romans 12 instructs us to offer our bodies as living sacrifices to God as an act of worship.[119] This tells me that my former view of worship was not what God intended. Our Sunday worship services and habitual acts of devotion, such as prayer and Bible-reading, are intended to shape us so that every moment of our lives is directed to bringing God the praise and honor He deserves.

Worship is more than an occasional obligation. God wants our lives to be acts of worship. We worship Him in the way we conduct ourselves at work, and can bring Him honor in the way we treat others. He is interested in our business affairs, our sex lives, our casual conversations, and our exercise routines. He loves us twenty-four hours a day, seven days a week, and He wants us to honor Him in a similar fashion.

Tithe. Tithing is a widely-acknowledged practice among Christians. The idea is that we must give a certain percentage of our income (usually ten percent) to God's Kingdom work. Some will argue for higher or lower percentages, and some will argue over how much of that should be given to local congregations, but the principle is that we should give.

This, as well as worship, can be seen as an obligation that is satisfied with minimal effort. I might believe that once I give my tithe to a worthy non-profit organization, my conscience can rest because I have fulfilled my duty. However, the idea that God wants only a portion from us can be misleading. If we think of tithing as fulfilling an obligation, we might be missing the point that everything we have belongs to God. The earth and everything in it belongs to Him;[120] He provides everything we have. Therefore, giving a portion of our wealth back to God should not be viewed as fulfilling a minimum contribution to pacify God but as an opportunity to give back to God a portion of what He gives to us.

Though God only asks us to give a portion back to Him, we must realize that everything we have belongs to Him. We must release everything to Christ in order to follow Him.

Have you ever approached repentance, faith, worship, or tithing from a minimalist perspective? Do you look for the least you can do in order to please God? If so, you are missing the fullness of what Christ has to offer you. He wants you to submit to Him completely so that you can experience the tremendous blessing He has in store for you.

The Really Good Day

All of this talk about the commitment Christ requires may cause many to think that they have to earn their salvation. One of the primary concepts that moved the Protestant Reformation forward was the teaching that we are justified by faith alone, not by our works. In this chapter, I have insisted that following Christ requires us to live and act differently. It may seem that my insistence contradicts the leaders of the Protestant Reformation (or the scripture on which they based their idea); for I am arguing that following Christ calls for a high level of commitment. I am telling you that your faith must be worked out in your actions. The teaching of justification by faith and the necessity for complete commitment do not contradict each other. Committing ourselves to Christ does not mean that we have earned our salvation or justified ourselves through good deeds.

Imagine a day in the future. You walk out to your mailbox and find three letters addressed to you. You take those letters inside, sit down at your kitchen table, and read them.

The first letter is from a local travel agency.

> Congratulations,
>
> You have been selected to receive an all-expense-paid trip to the Hawaiian Islands. This trip includes first-class airfare for you and one other person; a two-week stay at the hotel of your choosing on the Hawaiian Islands; vouchers for three meals per day at any restaurant on the islands; a free car rental during your stay; and free access to golf courses, theatres, museums, beaches and other forms of entertainment.
>
> In order to receive this free gift, you will need to take your driver's license or other valid picture ID to your local travel agency. At that time you will choose the dates for your travel.

FOLLOW THE LEADER

A smile comes across your face as you finish the letter. You have always wanted to travel to the Hawaiian Islands, but you did not think it would actually happen. Receiving this letter is like a dream come true.

You decide that you are having a good day.

You then open your second letter. It is in a standard business envelope from the Ford Motor Company.

> You have been selected to participate in a new pilot program for the Ford Motor Company. We are going to give you a brand new Ford vehicle of your choice.
>
> Please take this letter to your local Ford dealer. This letter will allow you to select any vehicle from that dealer's stock. We will pay for the tax, title, and license. We will even cover the cost of your vehicle insurance for the first year. In return you must fill out a questionnaire at the Ford dealership, detailing the reasons you selected your vehicle. The questionnaire should take about five minutes to complete.
>
> We hope that you will enjoy your new Ford vehicle for many years.

As you finish reading the letter, another smile comes across your face. Your car is in need of some major repairs, and you have been hoping to acquire a different one. You never thought it would be a new car, though just a few days earlier, you noticed the new Ford Excursions at your local dealer. You dreamed of driving one someday, but you never believed that day would come. Now, you will soon be driving a new car.

You decide that you are having a very good day.

The final letter is in a small, plain envelope on which your name and address are hand-printed. You don't recognize the writing, but you always save personal mail until all the other mail has been opened. Inside that envelope you find a certified check to you from your local bank that is written to you for $25,000. Accompanying that check you find this short, handwritten, unsigned note:

> Dear friend,
> I thought you could use this. Please take it to the bank, endorse it, and use the money as you see fit.

Now you conclude that this is the best day you have had in years.

Of course, you would realize that everything you received in the mail that day was unearned, since you did nothing to earn the Hawaiian trip, the new Ford Excursion, or the $25,000. Even though you might feel compelled to spend an entire day following up on these letters, you would still have not earned the gifts.

You would recognize the value of the gifts, and you would be grateful for the instructions. If the letter for the Hawaiian trip did not include instructions about how you were to secure your gift, you might conclude the offer was phony. Without the instructions in each letter, you might never follow up.

When Jesus calls us to complete commitment, He also promises wonderful gifts, complete with instructions. We receive the blessings He has in store for us by following Him with complete submission. It is a high calling, but our efforts in no way earn His grace. He gives us gifts, incredible gifts. Those gifts call for a high commitment. Those gifts are worth the commitment.

The instructions are wonderful, because those gifts are worthwhile. You would gladly spend a day traveling around town for a free vehicle, a trip to Hawaii, and $25,000. If those three letters had said I won a bumper sticker, a pack of gum, and a two-dollar coupon to my favorite restaurant, I probably would be inclined to throw those letters away. I wouldn't spend a day chasing those gifts.

The gifts Jesus has to give us are worthwhile. We could spend our entire lives pursing them, and we still could not say that we have earned them. Salvation, forgiveness, everlasting peace, fellowship with God, and eternity in paradise: these are gifts worth pursuing.

Total Commitment and Total Care

As our Master, Jesus calls for total commitment from us; we must give Him our all. Such commitment is difficult, but when we give it, Jesus satisfies our needs, heals our wounds, wipes our tears, and stills our worried hearts.

When my son Luke was five he learned that vehicles need gasoline to function. For two or three months, he expressed concern almost every time he got into our van. "Maybe we don't have enough gas," or "Do we need to stop at a gas station?" were words we heard constantly. One day my wife and I explained to him that we knew how much gas was in the van and that it was our job to worry about that. This reassurance seemed to free him from his worry. Once he was aware that his parents would watch over the gas situation, his concern was relieved. He understood that he was being cared for.

When we commit our lives to Christ, we can be sure that He cares for us. Like Luke, we can give up many concerns and fears about our futures. We can walk with the assurance that God will never leave us nor forsake us.[121] To illustrate the kind of peace and joy we can experience, I am going to conclude this chapter with a poem that compares following Christ to riding a bike.

The Road of Life[122]
At first, I saw God as my observer,
my judge,
keeping track of the things I did wrong,
so as to know whether I merited heaven
or hell when I die.
He was out there sort of like a president.
I recognized His picture when I saw it,
But I really didn't know Him

But later on
when I met Christ,

it seemed as thought life were rather like a bike ride,
but it was a tandem bike,
and I noticed that Christ
was in the back helping me pedal.

I don't know just when it was
that He suggested we change places,
but life has not been the same since.

When I had control,
I knew the way.
It was rather boring,
but predictable…
It was the shortest distance between two points.

But when He took the lead,
He knew delightful long cuts,
up mountains,
and through rocky places
at breakneck speeds,
it was all I could do to hang on!
Even though it looked like madness,
He said, "Pedal!"

I worried and was anxious
and asked,
"Where are you taking me?"
He laughed and didn't answer,
and I started to learn to trust.

I forgot my boring life
and entered into the adventure.
And when I'd say, "I'm scared,"
He'd lean back and touch my hand.

FOLLOW THE LEADER

He took me to people with gifts that I needed,
gifts of healing,
acceptance
and joy.
They gave me gifts to take on my journey,
my Lord's and mine.

And we were off again.
He said, "Give the gifts away;
they're extra baggage, too much weight."
So I did,
to the people we met,
and I found that in giving I received,
and still our burden was light.

I did not trust Him,
at first,
in control of my life.
I thought He'd wreck it;
but He knows bike secrets,
knows how to make it bend to take sharp corners,
knows how to jump to clear high rocks,
knows how to fly to shorten scary passages.

And I am learning to shut up
and pedal
in the strangest places,
and I'm beginning to enjoy the view
and the cool breeze on my face
with my delightful constant companion, Jesus Christ.

And when I'm sure I just can't do anymore,
He just smiles and says…"Pedal."

Questions for discussion/reflection:
How do convenient relationships differ with the relationship we are called to have with Christ?

Is Christ's grace free? Is it cheap? What is the difference?

What is the relationship between convenience in a relationship and intimacy in a relationship?

What is the difference between being a fan of Christ and a practitioner of faith?

Have you ever experienced a time in life when you believed God was steering while he called you to trust and pedal?

Chapter 6
Chasing Your Tail: The Futility of Following Yourself

Marcia did not like driving through big cities. The configuration of roads confused her and the logic behind the one-way streets escaped her. It did not take her long to get lost. For this reason, she rarely ventured into the city. She was content to travel in familiar circles.

One summer, Marcia's sister, who lived in Chicago, invited Marcia to come to a taping of the Oprah Winfrey show. This was an opportunity that could not be missed. Despite her fears and uncertainties about driving in the big city, Marcia decided that she would have to make this trip.

On the night before the taping of the Oprah show, Marcia left her home, just outside of the city, to go to her sister's house. She had been to her sister's house before, but she had never driven by herself. She was determined to make the trip.

After about thirty minutes of driving, Marcia hit a long stretch of road construction. Having decided to try a detour, she left the main highway and ventured into the urban streets that seemed so confusing.

You have probably already guessed that Marcia's detour did not turn out well. From her home the trip should have taken a total of ninety minutes. After leaving the highway, Marcia spent two hours driving up and down the maze of Chicago streets.

She finally had enough. She pulled over at a friendly looking gas station and used the pay phone to call her sister. Marcia began, "I need some help. I think I'm lost."

Her sister replied, "I live on the north side, just off of Lake Shore Drive."

"I know where you live, but I don't know how to get there."

"Where are you?"

"I'm at a gas station in Chicago. How do I get there from here?"

"I have to know where the gas station is!"

"How am I supposed to know where the gas station is? Didn't I tell you I'm lost?"

"If you want to know how to get here, I have to know where you are. Go outside and find the names of the nearest intersecting streets. Then call me back, and I will give you directions."

Marcia had to know where she was in order to find her destination. If she didn't understand her starting point, she could meander about the city for hours trying to stumble on to Lake Shore Drive. Once she knew her starting point, however, she could follow her sister's directions.

The Starting Point

Many people begin to follow Christ with a frame of mind that is similar to Marcia's. They know they are lost, they feel as though they have been wandering aimlessly, they believe Christ holds the answers to their dilemmas, and they correctly turn to Him. Their problem is they do not understand where they are starting from. If they could identify their starting point, however, they would have a better understanding of the journey.

Our starting point is a sinful nature which produces sinful thoughts and actions. If we do not understand that being human means that we struggle with sin, we might be fooled into believing that following Jesus is an easy process: He gives us directions, we follow the directions, and we reach our goal.

If we were perfect, following Jesus might be just that easy. Since we are not perfect, however, following is a complex task. In spite of Jesus' clear directions, some of us take wrong turns, others forget directions, or we take shortcuts that make us lose sight of our Lord.

We need to understand the weight of our own sin as we strive to follow Christ. Once we understand the nature of the problem, we can marvel at the power, love and patience of Christ as He leads us from death in sin to life in Him.[123]

A Two-Pronged Problem

Most people have a vague concept of sin. A young child with a basic knowledge of Christian teachings might describe sin as "doing bad things." Sin is telling lies, stealing, worshipping idols and engaging in other sorts of bad behavior. This is certainly true. Sin is a problem because we do bad things. This is the problem of guilt. We recognize sin because we have done things that are contrary to the Ten Commandments. When we sin, we hurt others and ourselves. The consequences of our actions are ruined reputations, ruined relationships, and the interruption of the orderliness God created.[124]

Sin is a problem that runs much deeper than the bad things we do, however. Sin is part of the fabric of our nature. It is a problem of corruption, a problem of the perverted disposition of our hearts. In his letter to the Romans, Paul describes sin as a living force that seems to infect our very being. It pulls us away from what is good and right and causes us to act against our better judgment, and do bad things.[125] The guilt is a symptom of a deeper problem.

Many people believe that if they merely stop doing bad things, they will solve the dilemma of sin. This solution is not possible because it does not repair the underlying cause of evil acts: a twisted disposition and corrupt heart.

Imagine a young mother going to her baby's crib one morning. She notices the baby has a runny nose. Somewhat concerned, she reaches to touch the baby's forehead and can feel that the baby has a fever. She rushes the baby to the doctor's office. Upon entering the examination room, the doctor asks, "What seems to be the problem?"

The mother replies, "My baby has a runny nose and is feverishly hot."

The doctor rubs his chin as he contemplates the problem and then says, "We can treat you baby very easily. For the runny nose, I will give you two small cotton balls. If you cram them in your baby's nose, it should stop running. For the high temperature, I suggest we cover your baby with ice. The temperature should drop quickly."

If any doctor suggested treating the symptoms of a runny nose and a fever with cotton balls and an ice pack, we would question his competence. Most parents understand that a runny nose and fever are symptoms for a deeper problem. If we simply plug up the nose and bring down the temperature, we have not addressed the deeper problem.

In the same way, if we think we can solve the mystery of sin by merely getting rid of our bad deeds, we are missing the deeper problem.

A Two-Part Solution

We can be thankful that Jesus responds to the problem of guilt and corruption with a two-part solution. He came to take away our guilt (the first problem) and the ultimate consequence of that guilt: eternity apart from God. Furthermore, He continues to work to resolve the deeper issue of the sinful nature living within us (the second problem).

Justification. Jesus removed the consequence of guilt by suffering for our sin on the cross. Many people have been justly punished by legal systems. Jesus' punishment was different, however, because He was innocent of any sin. He was never guilty because He kept God's law perfectly.[126] He always did the will of His Father. Even when He asked God to take the ultimate consequence of sin from Him, He qualified the request by stating that He was willing to submit to God's will, even though it meant that He had to suffer.[127]

Justification is a legal term. It means to settle a score or to make things right. A person who has been justified has been declared innocent by a legal authority, and His legal obligations have been satisfied. Once we commit a sin, we can never become innocent of it by our own actions. Justification is Christ's self-denying act of that accepting our punishment, so that He can legally declare us innocent. The consequence of sin has been taken away. Because of Christ's actions, God has forgiven our guilt and removes the consequence of our sin.

Sanctification. Even though justification takes away the guilt and consequences of sin, the problem of our sinful nature remains. Christ's work to restore us to a right relationship with God is only partially accomplished once we have been justified. Christ wants to make us new again, or wants to restore us to the perfection we possessed before sin entered the world and corrupted human nature. The process of making people new again is called sanctification.

Sanctification is a term that describes cleaning and restoring. A person who has been sanctified has been washed and is now able to enter the presence of the Holy One. The washing of sanctification is a process that makes us new.

When I think of sanctification, I think of people who restore classic vehicles. As a skilled auto restoration expert looks at a vintage car, he perceives its intrinsic value. Despite the dirt, dents, scratched paint, and the knocking sound in the engine, an auto expert sees the potential for complete restoration to its original beauty.

When Jesus sees us, He sees us with the eyes of an expert auto technician. Despite the guilt and corruption of sin, Christ sees the image of God in us. He works tirelessly to restore us to vintage condition. He sanctifies us.

This process of sanctification is not an instant process. Justification has been completed for those who follow Christ, solely because of what Christ accomplished on the cross. On the other hand, sanctification requires our participation. When Jesus calls us to a life of submission and obedience, He is telling us to cooperate in the Holy Spirit's work to make us new again. We cooperate with this work by following Christ.

The goal of sanctification is to make us perfect. Christ commands us to "Be perfect…as your Heavenly Father is perfect."[128] Though this may sound like a call to legalistically observe the laws and customs of the Old Testament, it is better viewed as an irresistible invitation to cooperate in God's work to restore you.

We start following Christ from the position of being guilty and corrupt. We come to Him out of need. Yet, we come to Him with great hope, because He is going to make us perfect. Sin is indeed a serious problem for all people. Followers of Christ come to Him with a deep sense of need. They realize that they need Him both to justify them for their guilt and to perfect their nature which has been corrupted by sin.

Works in Progress

Christ guarantees that His followers will experience eternity in God's presence. He describes a future with God as a joyful banquet or a priceless treasure. Even in difficult circumstances followers of Christ can have an enduring sense of peace that nothing will ever separate them from the love of God.[129]

Despite this guarantee we will still experience dissatisfaction in our walk with God. This dissatisfaction is not because God is unsatisfying, but because the corruption of sin continues to dwell in us. The promise of eternity gives us hope, but the experience of living in a sinful world can be frustrating. Furthermore, that sense of frustration multiplies as we grow in our realization that the corruption of sin still remains in our lives.

Following Christ is a life-long journey of being made new. The Bible tells us that "We…are being transformed into His likeness, with ever increasing glory."[130] As we are being made new, we have an uneasy sense that we are not yet where we are supposed to be.

We should not be surprised that even though we are being made new, we grow in the realization of our own shortcomings as we follow Christ. Christians can sometimes seem like a sour group, because they feel the burden of the need to confess and repent and the futility of trying to be better people, because sin seems to linger.

As we follow Christ, we might sometimes wonder, "Am I really being transformed into Christ's likeness? I seem to struggle with the same sins over and over." We might grow frustrated, because we expect people who have been saved to naturally live a life that is pleasing to God.

If you have ever had moments of doubt because you notice sin in your life, consider the possibility that you might not be getting more sinful, but rather, your growth in Christ might be causing you to recognize the depth of your sinfulness. When you walk with Christ, you begin to compare yourself to His perfection, and you see your own depravity.

Sam liked to run around with a rough crowd. He thought he was a pretty good guy because his life was much cleaner than theirs. Most of his co-workers cheated on their wives, lied to their supervisors, and drank too much alcohol. When Sam would cheat on his taxes, lie to his wife, or break promises to his children, he would ease his conscience by reasoning that he wasn't as bad as the guys he worked with.

Before a person knows Christ, he can, like Sam, pacify his conscience by comparing himself to others. Once we begin to follow Jesus, however, we change our point of comparison. We no longer pacified by the thought that we might be better than other people, because we are seeing our lives in comparison to Christ's.

It is possible for Christians to experience dissatisfaction in their walk with God because in God's presence, we notice sinfulness that we never recognized prior to a time when we followed Christ. We may experience seasons of life when we are overwhelmed by sin, but this does not necessarily mean we are getting worse. It might mean we are starting to see the depth of the sinful condition of our hearts.

In those moments of dissatisfaction, it is helpful for me to remember that God is not finished working in my life. Christ saw me at my worst, and was still willing to die and work to recreate me. My ongoing struggle is a reminder to me that He has not yet finished His work to restore me.

The Remnant

Although I am confident that Christ is working to restore me, I must also realize that I should not rest in my sinful condition. Because I am a feeble, sin-stained human, I should learn to be suspicious of myself. Even people who have been forgiven by Christ must realize that they will still struggle with sin. I have to realize that even my purest motives may be stained by my corrupt human nature. This is especially true when I am feeling the elation of following Christ. In those moments I am most prone to fool myself into thinking that my sinful nature is almost eradicated, and that I no longer need to worry about my self-deception.

If the truth were to be told, we would all have to confess that we love our sinful human nature. We know nothing else. We like the idea of being transformed into something better, but we would prefer that God leave certain aspects of our nature intact. We like pursuing our own desires, and the freedom to be our own masters. C.S. Lewis compares us to an honest man who pays his taxes. He is very willing to pay them, but he hopes that there is enough left for him to live on.[131] Similarly, we want Christ's Spirit to change us, but we also want to hold on to our old ways. As Christ transforms us, we hope the transformation is comparable to a haircut. We want to look better, but we want Him to only take a little off of the top.

Christ will not settle for a little off of the top, however. He intends to make us new. He is going to make us perfect. He is going to take our thoughts, deeds, and passions and make them subject to Him.

It is especially hard for us to let our passions go. Many believe if a person has a passion, it is automatically pure, and should not be questioned. The Bible, however, gives us a different perspective on passions. Passions can be aroused by the sinful world[132] and enslave us.[133] They are a part of us that Christ came to put to death.[134]

The word for passion in the New Testament is the same word as lust, which usually refers to an overwhelming sexual desire that can overpower a person's judgment. While many may believe passions are pure, they will realize that lust can have a power over a person that causes them to go astray. Even though our passions might not be sexual in nature, our desires can overwhelm us and lead us astray.

In the beginning of the book of Romans, we see how desires and passions can wreak havoc in the lives of people. In that book the apostle Paul describes a group of people who followed their own desires. As a consequence, God turned them over to those desires so that they could wallow in the misery that accompanied them.[135]

Even when we want to serve God, a remnant of the corruption of sin can ruin our best efforts. When I first became a pastor, I was shocked to learn of the number of scandalous events that caused pastors to leave ministry. It was all too frequent that a pastor had to leave his office due to sexual sins.

I do not believe that most men who aspire to become pastors do so in order to pick up women. I do believe, however, that people who are striving to become leaders in the church fall under the impression that they no longer struggle with worldly desires. They no longer suspect themselves; and therefore they do not guard their hearts. They allow feelings and passions develop, sometimes from intentions that were absolutely innocent, and they fall.

Christ taught His disciples to pray that they would be kept from temptation. I think the language of the Lord's Prayer is significant. In the final request of that prayer, Jesus teaches us to pray, "lead us not into temptation, but deliver us from the evil one."[136] The prayer was not that we should be strong enough to overcome temptation, but that God would lead us in ways that avoid temptation altogether.

We should avoid temptation because we are weak. If we are exposed to enough temptation, sooner or later we will fail. This request means that those who struggle with alcoholism should not think they are strong enough to sit in a bar with their friends and not drink, they should stay away. The man and woman who are dating and infatuated with each other should not deceive themselves into believing they can be alone in a bedroom without engaging in sexual intercourse. They should be aware of their tendency to sin and should avoid situations that could lead them astray.

Sometimes our passions may seem innocent or indifferent. I might have a passion for flying kites or riding bikes. As far as I know, God's word does not prohibit us from these kinds of activities. If our seemingly innocent passions lead us away from Christ, however, we should let them go. Jesus told His followers that if their right hand offends them, they should cut it off.[137] Jesus had nothing against right hands; but He did not want anything to interfere with their efforts to follow Him.[138]

When we realize that our starting point is a condition of sinful corruption, we must also understand that even though we are being transformed, the remnant of our sinful nature will rear its ugly head if we do not keep it in check.

Striving and Stumbling

Christ calls His followers to be perfect. We do not meet that standard, at least not yet. Sincere Christians stumble as they walk with God. We find ourselves frustrated and struggling, because we do things that we wish we wouldn't do. Once we recognize where we are coming from, however, we are less likely to believe that we will be quickly and easily made perfect.

The process of being made new is similar to a surgery. A few years ago my father underwent a hip-replacement surgery. For months he had been experiencing pain in his leg. The surgery was successful, but it took him a long time to recover. He had difficulty walking, he needed assistance for many things, and in some ways he was in worse condition after the surgery than before. He had to endure physical therapy, which is extensive exercising to help a body gain strength. The surgery corrected the problem that caused pain, but Dad still had to gain strength. While Dad was enduring physical therapy, he experienced times of weakness, and was prone to stumble and fall. He also had to unlearn bad habits that had developed because of the pain that existed prior to the surgery. Therapy brought healing and strength, and it helped his body to adjust to the corrections that were made through surgery.

Because of Christ's work in my life, I consider myself a recipient of a spirit transplant. Christ has breathed new life into me, and the old ways are fading away. By taking the consequences of my guilt upon Himself, He gave me an opportunity for new life. Now I must learn how to live with this new spirit. Like my dad after his surgery, I am enduring a long process of recovery. I believe this is a process that will continue until Christ's brings the fullness of His Kingdom. The prescribed therapy for this spirit transplant is following Christ: I obey Him and imitate Him. Through this therapy of following, Christ is training me and shaping me for the future.

As I endure this spiritual therapy, I often find the recovery to be a frustrating and difficult process. The main difficulty is that my sinful nature continues to desire what is contrary to the Spirit.[139] My old habits and ways of living continue to be automatic responses when I enter stressful times. I do not want to be self-centered, but in busy weeks, I sometimes fall into patterns of ignoring people around me so that I can accomplish my goals. The corruption of sin threatens to pull me back into old ways of living; it attempts to reject my newly transplanted spirit.

I stumble and fail in other ways as I gain strength through following Christ. I am forgetful, I am rather unorganized, and I often take on more obligations than I am capable of keeping. These weaknesses continue to plague me, even though I have received a new spirit through Christ. I sometimes pray that God will make me perfectly whole, but my flaws seem to cause me to stumble.

Sometimes these personality flaws cause hardships in my relationships with others. I grow in my frustration because I think I should be getting better. "After all," I reason, "I have been forgiven and I am trying to follow Christ. Why am I still forgetful and unorganized?"

Although followers of Christ possess a new spirit, they still struggle with weaknesses in their natures. Some of those weaknesses hardly qualify as sinful. The Bible does not say, "Thou shalt not be unorganized." However, these weaknesses cause pain and struggle in our lives.

It is not easy to walk through life as a follower of Christ. We have been forgiven by Christ, and we are assured that we will be made perfect. But in the process of becoming perfect, we continue to stumble and fall. Despite our struggles, we continue to press on, realizing that this is a long recovery process. Following Christ is not a short sprint. It is a marathon. We continue to put one foot in front of another as we pursue the goal of perfection.[140]

The Problem of Hypocrisy[141]

As we follow Christ, we grow in strength and peace. Our lives will change noticeably. One of the difficulties for people who are traveling from a starting point of corruption and guilt is that they want to appear as though they have made monumental progress in their journey when they have really just started. Christians are prone to pretend that they are better than they actually are. This is the problem of hypocrisy.

Most people would probably tell you that hypocrisy is to "say one thing and do another." Though this is often true, it is not a fair definition of hypocrisy. When I was nine years old, I tried to use my bike to propel myself over a ramp. I fell and chipped a tooth. If I tell my sons today that it can be dangerous to jump your bike over a ramp, am I being a hypocrite? By the common definition (say one thing and do another), the answer would be yes. According to the common definition, anyone who admits a mistake is automatically guilty of being a hypocrite, because they are advising others not to do what they have done.

The word "hypocrite" is from a Greek word which means actor. Early in my studies of the Greek New Testament, I had a difficult time understanding how the concepts of hypocrisy and acting are related. I had accepted the common conception of hypocrisy, and acting did not fit that concept.

Actors portray characters other than themselves. When I go to the movies and watch Tom Hanks play a character, I realize that he is acting. I do not believe that Tom Hanks has ever been stranded on a deserted island, played college football, or ascended to the top of the Empire State Building to meet a woman. In his movies he is taking on a character and playing a role.

Like Tom Hanks, hypocrites take on roles to appear different from what they are. They pretend to be organized and thoughtful when they are not. They might pretend to have wonderful times of devotions, though they do not. They will tell stories describing their patience, and intentionally neglect to tell you about the times they have erupted with anger for trivial reasons. The difference between Tom Hanks and a hypocrite is that Tom Hanks does not intend to fool other people into thinking he is actually someone else. A hypocrite does want to fool others.

Christians can be hypocritical, because we want to make progress as we follow Christ. We want to get better and be free from the struggles of our sinful nature. As we recognize the depth of sin in our lives, we are tempted to hide it and act as though we do not struggle with sin. We try to make others think we "have it together."

Even sincere people can be guilty of hypocrisy. We might even fool ourselves into believing we are better than we are. This is one more reason why it is so important to know our starting point. When we begin the life-transforming process of following Christ, we begin a process that will end in our perfection. However, that transformation will not be instantaneous. We will continue to struggle with our guilt and with our corruption. If we pretend that sin no longer has an impact on our lives, we are deceiving ourselves.[142]

An Undivided Heart

"Give me an undivided heart"[143] is the prayer of the author of Psalm 86. The author of this prayer realizes that the problem in our lives is more than just our location. At the beginning of this chapter, I told you a story about Marcia, who was lost in a big city. Actually, Marcia's problem was not merely her location. She also had a poor sense of direction. Even if her sister could give her clear directions, she would probably get lost again.

Just as Marcia was in a difficult situation, so are we. Marcia was lost, and was hampered by her inability to navigate larger metropolitan areas. She was directionally challenged. Left to our own devices, we are spiritually lost. Sin is a multi-faceted problem in our lives. It leaves us lost, unable to find God, and it gives us a terrible sense of direction.

We naturally have divided hearts—hearts that are unaware of the severity of their condition. We are torn between the desire to please God and to satisfy our own desires. This division of loyalties is at the heart of our problem. When we see the division within our hearts, we realize that we need Christ's intervention. Do we have the good sense to stop and ask for directions like Marcia did? Do we have the wisdom to ask God for undivided hearts like the Psalmist does?

When we set our hearts on following Christ, He gently guides us out of the chaos of our sinned-stained lives, and begins to transform our divided, deceptive hearts in order to make us perfect.

Questions for discussion/reflection:
What is the difference between being guilty and being corrupt?

Why do we need to be justified?

How does sanctification change our status with God?

Should mature Christians be suspicious of themselves? Why or why not?

How does hypocrisy interfere with following Christ?

Chapter 7
Playing Copycat

Directionally-challenged people need very concrete, simple steps to follow.

If you just finished reading the last chapter, you might be feeling somewhat depressed. You have just been reminded that you are guilty, corrupt, consumed with your own desires, and prone to be a hypocrite.

How do directionally-challenged people get out of this mess? We need very concrete and simple steps to follow.

The Bible gives followers of Christ simple, concrete instructions. "Be imitators of God."[144] "Your attitude should be the same as that of Christ Jesus."[145] These instructions tell us to copy Christ. Followers do not just go where Christ leads; they also do what Christ does.

God knows our hearts better than we know them. He knows how to lead us out of the sinful condition that plagues us and into His perfection. He calls us to cooperate in that process by imitating Jesus.

The Way We Learn

It was game two of the 1991 NBA Finals. The Chicago Bulls had never won an NBA championship, and they were playing the Los Angeles Lakers, winners of 5 championships in the previous decade. The Bulls had lost game one on a heartbreaking shot in the final seconds.

In game two, Michael Jordan executed one of the prettiest basketball moves I have ever witnessed. He took a pass at the top of the key, dribbled, and jumped from just inside the free throw line. As he jumped, he carried the ball in his right hand, and it looked as though he was going to throw down a thunderous tomahawk-style dunk. To everyone's surprise, in midair Jordan transferred the ball from his right hand to his left, contorted his body, and gently laid the ball off of the backboard for a left-handed lay-up. As I watched this play unfold before my eyes, my jaw dropped. I had never seen anything like this original move. As the announcers searched for words to describe the play, I realized that I had just seen something that would be long-remembered.

The Bulls went on to win that game and that series for their first of six championships in the 1990s. That summer I began to see people on basketball courts everywhere trying to imitate Michael's game-two move. Gatorade even developed an advertising campaign that showed children on outdoor basketball courts trying to copy Jordan's incredible shot. As the children played, a song described the longing of those children (and many watching the commercial) to "be like Mike."[146]

In the world of sports, people try to imitate their favorite athletes. They learn as they try to copy the moves, mannerisms, and style of their favorite stars. Famous basketball players will tell you that they honed their skills as children by copying the moves of their favorite players. That process of imitation helped them to learn and eventually to develop moves of their own.

Followers of Christ are called to learn from Christ as they imitate Him. Imitation teaches us how we should follow Christ, and it also gives us practice doing His will.

Throughout most of my years of school I learned through organized lectures in a very structured and controlled classroom setting. The teacher told me what I needed to know; I memorized the pertinent information; and I proved that I had learned by taking a test. That was not a bad system for learning. I liked having people tell me what I needed to know. However, this is not the only way to learn.

Remember, Jesus' followers were his students. Up to this point in our book we have talked about the commitment of following. In this chapter we are talking about the way we learn. Jesus seems to use a method for teaching that might be unfamiliar to many.

In 2002 I met Master Jason Lee. Master Lee holds an eight-degree black belt in Tae Kwon Do. I asked him to teach me, and he was willing. I was struck by the way he taught because I received so little verbal instruction. After a fellow student told me how to wear my white belt, Master Lee gently scolded me for standing in the area designated for students who had attained the rank of black-belt. As class began, Master Lee recited some words in Korean that I did not understand. The other students seemed to know what they were doing, so I copied them. After ten minutes I started to understand that my role was simply to imitate. I did the same stretching exercise that the others were doing. When the others did pushups and sit-ups, I did pushups and sit-ups. I tried to perform the same kicks and punches that Master Lee and the other students were executing. After thirty minutes of class, another student took me aside and gave a brief time of personal instruction.

Tae Kwon Do provides many benefits; among them are physical conditioning and the ability to defend oneself. I learned something else: that we learn in a variety of ways. After completing elementary school, middle school, high school, college, and seminary, I had begun to think that the primary way we learn is by listening to other people and committing what they say to memory. Now I understand differently. Through practicing Tae Kwon Do, I realized that one of the primary ways we learn is through imitating. Certainly, there have been times when Master Lee has given me verbal instruction. When Master Lee offers verbal instruction, he usually intends it to help me reflect on what I have been practicing. He makes corrections as I learn.

Much of what we learn comes through the practice of imitating others. I never sat down and verbally instructed my sons on how to use a spoon. They simply started copying me at the dinner table. The children who imitated Michael Jordan's famous move in the 1991 NBA Finals did not attend a class on aerial contortions. They simply imitated what they saw. Imitation is a powerful way of learning.

Jesus' Classroom

Jesus developed His disciples into church leaders by having them imitate Him. In Luke 9 -10 we see a wonderful example of Jesus' giving His disciples on-the-job training. After they had followed Him and learned from Him for a period of time, He sent them out on their own. Luke 9 begins with Jesus' instruction to go out and proclaim the kingdom of God and heal the sick.[147] If I had been one of the original disciples, this instruction would have caused me a great deal of discomfort. I might have said, "Excuse me, but I do not remember that you taught us how to heal the sick. Was I absent the day we covered that?" These disciples had never done anything like that before, yet, with minimal instruction He sent them out.

In spite of the difficult task, the disciples experienced success in their assignments. A crowd followed them, and Herod, the ruler of the region, heard reports of their activities. Jesus may not have given specific instructions, but the disciples were able to experience success because they went out with His power, and they had learned by watching Him. This trip was a mission of imitating what they had seen Jesus do.

After the disciples returned and reported to Jesus what had happened, He led them to a place where they could be by themselves in order to discuss their on-the-job training.[148] As we will see in the rest of chapter 9, the experience of being sent out triggered a readiness within the disciples to learn new things about Jesus and His ministry. Once the disciples had the experience of imitating Him, Jesus wanted to take them aside to reflect quietly on their mission trip.

The crowds, however, had different ideas. They followed Jesus and His disciples because they wanted to be near the healers and teachers of the Kingdom. Jesus did not disappoint them, but He spent most of that day teaching and healing.

Later in the day the disciples encouraged Jesus to send the crowds away so that they could get food. Jesus turned this into another opportunity for more on-the-job training. He gave the disciples an implausible command, "You give them something to eat."[149] This time the disciples balked. How could they feed such large crowds? They could handle preaching and healing, in fact, they had just had a successful internship doing exactly that. But this business of feeding large crowds seemed to be too much. Jesus took matters into His own hands. He separated the crowds into groups and turned a small meal into a feast for thousands.

Jesus' process for training His disciples caused them to see Him in a new way. Through imitating Christ, they were now ready to learn more, and Jesus began to reveal Himself to them in new ways.

Intimate Truth Revealed

The gospel of Luke tells us that immediately after He fed the crowds, Jesus questioned His disciples about His identity. Peter confessed that Jesus was the Christ of God.[150] This was the first time in Luke that a human being identified Jesus as the Christ. Because of their experiences imitating Jesus, the disciples were now ready to learn more about His identity. Their on-the-job training prepared them for a deeper knowledge of their leader.

Jesus did not stop by merely allowing His disciples to understand that He was the promised Messiah of the Old Testament. In this intimate time of talking, He also began to reveal the nature of His work; that He had come to suffer and die, even though He was the promised Messiah.

Try to imagine how the disciples might have felt at that moment, because this must have been an incredibly confusing time for them. In a very short period, they had personally preached and healed, seen Jesus miraculously feed thousands, and learned that their teacher was the promised Messiah. After all of these promising developments, their teacher told them that He was going to suffer and die. It must have seemed like a roller coaster ride. Furthermore, Jesus added that if they were going to follow Him, they would have to be prepared to suffer as well.[151]

Immediately following their time of imitating Christ's ministry, the disciples learned secrets of the Kingdom that they had not previously understood. Through imitating Christ they were prepared to develop a deeper, more intimate relationship with Him. Jesus made it clear that the things He shared with them were not to be told too quickly. Although the disciples had followed and imitated, the world had not. Therefore, the world was not yet ready to hear these truths about Jesus.

Mountain-Top Experience

The fast pace of Luke 9 continues. After Jesus revealed Himself as the promised Messiah,[152] He ascended a mountain with three disciples, where they witnessed a revelation of Christ's glory and the return of Moses and Elijah.[153] On that mountain top, God confirmed that Christ's followers should listen to Jesus, even though Christ was saying some hard things about suffering. Despite their incredible success in preaching and healing, Jesus and His followers would suffer.

Even though God confirmed Christ's words, Jesus' disciples were caught up in the apparent success of His ministry. Jesus was leading large crowds, healing diseases, and serving feasts for thousands from a small snack. Why wouldn't the disciples be confident about their future? What had they seen that would indicate to them that suffering was a part of their path? One can hardly blame the disciples if the talk about suffering went right past them. They were experiencing an incredible time of seeing Christ's glory revealed.

Their actions proved that they did not grasp the reality of Christ's suffering. The disciples argued over who was the greatest.[154] After Christ had told them of His suffering, they still could think only about the future success. The disciples also began to display a bit of arrogance regarding their position. One suggested that others who ministered in Jesus' name should be stopped, since they were not part of the elite group.[155] On another occasion, the disciples then became angry because of the opposition Christ received in Samaria. Two of them suggested that they could call down fire to destroy those who would not welcome Him.[156]

This must have been a frustrating time for Jesus. His disciples were not listening to Him because they were blinded by their dreams of future success and their place in the Messiah's Kingdom. In the final section of Luke 9 Jesus emphasized that there was a cost to following Him.[157] He warned that following Him was not a life of comfort and ease; He did not issue a call to be observed only when it was convenient. Following Christ has always been a difficult call to a path that will bring suffering.

It seems as though Luke shaped this section of His gospel to show us how things changed for Christ's disciples once they imitated Him. After their successful ministry expedition in the beginning of Luke 9, they witnessed Jesus feeding crowds, they saw His glory revealed on a mountain, and they even heard a confirmation that He is the promised Christ. With this good news came Christ's revelation that following Him would be costly. He would have to suffer and die. His followers would be called to give up everything to follow Him, and they, too, would suffer.

In the beginning of Luke 10 Jesus sends His disciples on another ministry trip. This time, He sends more than just the twelve we are familiar with. Seventy-two go on this trip, and Jesus gives them more extensive information from Jesus about what to expect. Once His disciples had endured the initial training, and the revelation that they would suffer, Christ was prepared to give them a fuller explanation of His ministry, and how to respond to suffering and rejection. His disciples had grown through the process of imitating Jesus.

Christ does not call His followers to be mere observers. He calls us to participate in His plans. As we learn through imitation, he slowly nurtures us to become more like Him.

The Intimacy of Imitating

Imitation produces two primary results. First, it changes you in some way. By imitating another person, you begin to take on his characteristics and become more like him. When I imitate my Tae Kwon Do instructor, I grow in my skills and abilities. Through practicing his actions, I am changed.

The second effect of imitating is developing a closer bond with the one you imitate. When I was younger, I used to laugh at my father's sleeping habits. He would wake up very early in the morning, usually before five o'clock am. After working all day as a bricklayer, he would come home, get cleaned up, and promptly lie down on the couch, where he would fall asleep. Once supper was ready, he would get off of the couch to eat, and after our family devotions, he would immediately return to his position on the couch. He often watched television, but everyone in our house knew that it was only a matter of time before Dad would be sleeping again. Most nights, I went to bed while my dad was still sleeping on the couch. I learned that he would usually wake up around 1:00 or 2:00 am so that he could go to bed. This pattern seemed very odd to me. I did not understand why he wanted to sleep so much. Furthermore, if he wanted to sleep, why would he sleep on the couch until 2:00 am, only to wake up and go to bed?

My perspective changed after I graduated from high school. During the summer before I attended college, I worked on a construction site with bricklayers. The work was physically demanding, and I found I needed more sleep than I had been accustomed to getting. After a month of working, I noticed there was something familiar about my daily routine. I would wake up in the morning, usually before 5:00 am, work hard all day, come home, and take a shower. After my shower I would take a short nap on the couch. I always got up to have dinner with my family. Although I often had friends invite me to join them for some fun, I was too tired; so after dinner, I usually settled for watching television. I would fall asleep watching the television, and at about 11:00 pm I would wake up and go to bed.

When Dad exercised his sleeping pattern, I thought it was strange because I did not understand. I thought he just liked to choose unique sleeping patterns. Once I imitated His work, however, I learned more about his daily routine. I found that the physical work of mixing mortar, carrying brick, and building scaffolding required me to sleep very much, as my father did. By doing what my dad did, I learned more about him.

Furthermore, because I had followed in my dad's footsteps, I understood the frustrations and pleasures of construction work. I knew more about the building process, and this gave us more common ground for discussions. I grew closer to him by imitating him.

When we imitate Christ, we grow nearer to Him. That is what happened to the disciples in Luke 9. They copied His ministry, and as a result they learned much more about Him. As He revealed Himself to them, they started to grow in their understanding of who He was and what He came to do.

The Boldness of Intimacy

When we imitate Christ, we grow closer to Him, and we begin to understand His purposes more clearly. Through Christ we are also blessed to experience greater intimacy with the Father. With that greater intimacy we grow in boldness to approach our Father. When we first learn who God is and what He does, the thought of approaching Him can be frightening. When Isaiah was first ushered into God's presence, He cried out[158] because he was terrified by the majesty of God. Proverbs tells us that the fear of the Lord is the beginning of wisdom.[159] When we first enter God's presence, it is appropriate to respond with fear. He is an almighty and holy God. If His anger would burn against us, we would have no hope. As we get to know Him more fully, however, we discover the blessing of confidence in His presence.

This confidence does not come from the development of our own skills. Rather, it comes from the reassurance of knowing how much God loves us. He went to great lengths to secure our salvation, giving His own son. From the time Adam and Eve first sinned, God had a plan to redeem His people.[160] When we imitate Christ and get to know God more intimately, we discover His tremendous love for us. Why would someone set a plan in motion from the beginning of time to save people who had rebelled against Him? The only explanation is His love.

As we serve others, we begin to see them through the eyes of God. We notice their gifts and abilities. We develop an appreciation for their unique characteristics. We begin to treasure them as image bearers of God. This realization comes as we imitate Christ in our service. Through imitation, we grow in our confidence of God's love for us. We no longer have to approach Him as fearful children, but we can boldly enter His presence.[161]

After walking with God for some time, Abraham was able to make bold requests. God told Abraham that He was going to destroy the cities of Sodom and Gomorrah.[162] When standing in the presence of the all-powerful God who was about to destroy two cities, most people would cower with fear. I believe my natural instinct would have been to run away with relief, thankful that God did not want to destroy me! I do not think I would have wanted to risk making God angry with me by begging Him to alter His plans. Abraham, however, knew God more fully because he had walked with God, developing an intimacy with Him. Abraham understood God's love; he knew God had favored him. Therefore, he believed that God would not become unjustly angry, if he boldly requested God to spare the city if only fifty righteous people lived there. Once God agreed, Abraham pushed even further, eventually getting God to say that He would spare the cities for the sake of only ten righteous people. In this way, Abraham was able to approach God boldly because He had developed an intimate walk with Him.

Moses also felt free to approach God boldly. Although the people of Israel followed God as He led them and performed many miracles, they rebelled against God.[163] Therefore, God became weary, and told Moses that He was ready to destroy these people and make a new nation with Moses. This was undoubtedly a difficult spot for Moses. He was talking with the all-powerful God who had destroyed the Egyptian armies. Moses had seen His anger burn against a whole nation; he knew what God could do. Most people would think it foolish to speak against the plans of an angry God. Not Moses. He pleaded with God to spare Israel.

Jesus seems to admire bold persistence. When a Canaanite woman asked Jesus to heal her daughter, he initially denied her, saying He was sent to save the lost sheep of Israel.[164] Jesus explained that He would not take bread from the children of Israel and toss it to the dogs, meaning the Canaanites. The woman persisted, saying that she wanted only crumbs that fell from the children's table. Jesus was impressed and praised the woman for her great faith. This faith was demonstrated by an act of bold persistence. This woman approached Jesus with a request, and when she was denied, she persisted.

Followers of Christ have the privilege of boldly approaching God's throne. The intimacy that we develop through imitating is a blessing, because through it we become confident that God loves us. Although we may begin our walk with Him with a holy fear, we realize His love for us as we grow nearer to Him, and we receive the blessing of a faith that is confident and bold in His presence.

The Art of Imitating

For argument's sake, let's assume that you are convinced. Let's assume that you want to be an imitator of Christ. You might be thinking, "I would like to imitate Christ, but I don't believe He has called me to preach the Kingdom and heal. I am glad that His disciples performed miracles, but how does He want me to imitate Him?" Most people will not imitate Christ by performing miracles and teaching. You might not view this as your calling, but that does not exempt you from imitating Christ as you follow Him.

The book of Philippians gives us a good starting point for imitating Christ: "Your attitude should be the same as that of Christ Jesus."[165] Throughout His life Jesus demonstrated an attitude of willingness to serve. He emptied Himself, giving up His rightful position in heaven and humbling Himself so that He could serve others.

Before Jesus died, He took His disciples to an upper room for the Last Supper. In that room, the divine Teacher became a servant and stooped to wash the dirty feet of His student followers.[166] He had every right to demand one of those disciples to wash His feet, but Jesus did not demand what was rightfully His.

Today people are intent on receiving what they view as their rights, and they become very frustrated when their rights are denied or impeded. Jesus stood in sharp contrast to that natural instinct. He did not insist on having His rights enforced; nor did He complain that He was entitled to better treatment. He came to serve, so that we might live.

Even the act of forgiving is an act of forfeiting one's rights. Occasionally we have legitimate reasons to be angry with others, and sometimes we are innocent victims of another person's schemes. When a husband leaves his wife and children to be with another woman, the forsaken wife has every right to be angry because she has been wronged. Jesus did not teach us that we should never be angry or that we are wrong for feeling hurt. Forgiveness is not a denial of anger and hurt. Rather it is an act of acknowledging that damage has been done and then forfeiting your right to be angry and demand revenge. Christ Himself demonstrated this on the cross when He prayed that His Father would forgive those who persecuted Him.[167]

Jesus called us to imitate His work as by forgiving others. He even taught us to pray, "Forgive us our debts, as we also have forgiven our debtors."[168] These words clearly establish a link between forgiving others and being forgiven. As we imitate Christ, we must forgive others, just as He forgave others—and just as He has forgiven us.

After Jesus washed the feet of His disciples, He charged them to imitate Him. We might understand this in principle, but putting it into practice can cause a problem. We often struggle to imitate someone else, because there is something awkward about taking another person's actions and trying to perform them. When you see a young child on the playground trying to imitate a Michael Jordan performance, you will notice the maneuver is not as polished as it was when it was originally performed. New moves and maneuvers do not come easily. It takes humility to imitate someone, because we will struggle with apparent failure. As we attempt to imitate others, we will realize that it is often difficult to do something that someone else seems to do effortlessly.

Jesus seemed to forgive with ease. Before He healed, he would simply proclaim that sins were forgiven. When I am legitimately angry at someone, forgiving is much more difficult. I might be able to say the words, "I forgive you," but forfeiting my right to be angry is another matter. I tend to mull over the way in which I was wronged. I fight the temptation to plot some kind of revenge, and struggle to treat kindly the person I have forgiven. I have to spend a lot of time in prayer asking

God to change my demeanor towards someone who has hurt me, because forgiveness is difficult.

Similarly, I often feel awkward when I try to serve someone. If I am truly acting selflessly, I should not expect him to notice my efforts, yet I feel put off if my efforts are not acknowledged. I sincerely want to serve others, as Christ did, but it seems awkward. Yet awkwardness is part of any learning experience. Feeling awkward should not keep us from attempting to imitate Christ. Awkwardness is not a sign that we are failing in our efforts to imitate Christ. It means we are not perfect yet. Awkwardness is an indication that we need to keep trying.

Imitating Christ is an art. An artist usually gets her start by learning the basic fundamentals of her craft. A painter will study the use of color and brushing techniques. She will practice replicating a variety of images in an attempt to gain skill. She might begin learning the art form by copying other works of art, or even try painting by numbers to refine her use of color. Some of her first paintings might not be very good, but after much time and painstaking effort, she will see improvement. The painter will then attempt to create more intricate pieces of art. As we imitate Christ, we start by adopting His attitude of humble service. We struggle to forgive others, and labor to find time to pray. We may stumble over our words as we tell a friend about His saving work. In short, imitating Christ might not feel natural, and it might seem as though we are painting by the numbers to do as Christ did. We may not feel as if we are doing anything original, but we are being shaped by Christ's grace.

Imitating vs. Pretending

The call to imitate Christ can leave Christians open to the accusation of hypocrisy. In the previous chapter, I defined a hypocrite as an actor, someone who tries to portray an image that is different from reality. Wouldn't imitating Christ open us to the charge of hypocrisy? As we imitate Christ, aren't we trying to be something we are not?

Hypocrisy is a serious problem in the Christian church. Some people who claim to be followers of Christ are merely acting so that others will think highly of them. For these actors, following Christ is nothing more than acting in front of a crowd so that others will offer them social privileges. Church leaders, who publicly denounce the evils of pornography by day, might hurry home to their computers at night to view the very thing they denounce. These people might speak publicly against evil as a means to keep others from suspecting their inner struggle. They do not want their character to be revealed by the light.

Hypocrites try to hide the stain of sin in their lives and portray a positive public image. They are trying to make other people think that they are something that they are not. They want people to think they are righteous and holy, when inwardly they are neither interested in righteousness nor holiness. They are putting on a show; acting in order to make an impression on others. They are more worried about managing their image than they are about growing in their intimacy with Christ.

These people are doing something different from those who are trying to imitate Christ. Imitators of Christ will also act against their natural inclinations, in ways that are not consistent with their feelings, but this is not hypocrisy.

C.S. Lewis challenges followers of Christ to pretend to be like Jesus in order to become more like Him.[169] This kind of imitating is not hypocrisy. As we pretend to be like Jesus, we will discover an awkward struggle to be like Him. It is an unnatural struggle, but that does not mean it is hypocrisy. When I feel tired and cranky, I should still try to treat others with kindness. Some would say that I am being inauthentic or hypocritical for being agreeable when I am in a bad mood. On the contrary, if I am able to deny my natural inclinations to treat others rudely, I am imitating Christ. I may be awkward and imperfect in my imitation, I will undoubtedly fail to treat others with perfect kindness, and I might even slip and allow my annoyance to seep through, but when I am trying to imitate Christ, I am being faithful to His challenge.

The difference between hypocrisy and imitation lies in the motivation. The hypocrite will try to appear better than she actually is, but the imitator of Christ will aspire to be better than she currently is.

Because imitators of Christ try to act like Christ, they might be vulnerable to the accusation of hypocrisy. When we pretend in order to practice becoming more like Christ, however, and when we are interested in a transformed life rather than a mere appearance of righteousness, our pretending is not hypocrisy.

Blessings of Imitating

If you have ever ridden a bike on a windy day, you know it can be difficult to fight the wind. Bikers who ride together have learned how to minimize the effects of the wind: they follow each other in a straight line. When they do this, the first biker creates a draft, which pulls the other bikers with him as he cuts a path in the wind. This draft makes pedaling easier for the other bikers. Followers of Christ get the benefit of riding behind their Leader. Christ creates a draft. When we imitate Him, we gain the blessings of His efforts, and we get to go where He leads.

Jesus told His followers to humble themselves, as He did. He told them that when they attend a banquet, they should not take the seat of honor.[170] Instead, they should sit in the worst seat available. If they were to sit in a seat of honor, they would be embarrassed when the host moved them. But if they take the worst seat, they would be honored when they host brought them to a better place. In Philippians 2, Paul encouraged the followers of Christ to imitate His humility by giving up their rights. Our model is Christ, who was obedient to the point of suffering and dying on the cross. He did not take the seat of honor but accepted the scorn and shame of sin. After Paul describes Christ submission, he notes that God lifted Him to glory.[171] He humbly submitted, and the Host, the Creator of the Heavens and the earth, lifted Him to the highest possible seat of honor.

When we imitate Christ, we ride in the draft of His momentum, following Him in humble submission. We may suffer scorn and shame because of Him, but we endure it with full confidence that His momentum will pull us through the headwinds of sin and into His perfect glory.

Questions for discussion/reflection:
What are some basic life skills that we only learn by imitating?

Why did Jesus wait so long to reveal His suffering to the disciples?

What is the relationship between imitating Christ and being able to approach Christ with boldness?

Describe a time when you felt awkward as you tried to imitate Christ.

What is the difference between imitating Christ and hypocrisy?

Chapter 8
The Metamorphosis of the Chase

In the movie "The Karate Kid"[172] Daniel LaRusso learns lessons of life from the handyman in his apartment building, Mr. Miyagi. After Mr. Miyagi rescues Daniel from a fight with a local gang of thugs, Daniel asks Mr. Miyagi to teach him how to defend himself. Mr. Miyagi agrees, but before training starts, he insists that Daniel must perform some chores. Daniel spends days working for Mr. Miyagi, painting a fence, waxing cars, and sanding wooden floors. He does not mind working to pay for his karate lessons, but after all of his work, he believes that he should have had at least one lesson. Finally, Daniel shows his frustration. He believes he has become a slave for Mr. Miyagi. He wants to learn karate, but he thinks he is wasting his time doing chores.

After Daniel's outburst, Mr. Miyagi calmly explains that Daniel had already learned a great deal about karate. He shows Daniel that the motions he had been repeating by painting, sanding, and waxing are the motions used to defend oneself in karate. For viewers of this movie, this is an eye-opening scene. Before this, they have felt sympathetic toward Daniel, because it seems as though Mr. Miyagi has been taking advantage of a young man who wants to learn from him. Now, however, they realize that all of Daniel's work has been purposeful. It was not merely a prerequisite for training; it was the beginning of his training.

Daniel did not understand the nature of his jobs. He thought that he had to pay Mr. Miyagi for future lessons and that he would do some odd jobs for his payment. While Mr. Miyagi certainly benefited from the chores that Daniel performed, his intention was not merely payment; it was training. The repetitive motions of the jobs were a foundational part of Daniel's training.

Like Daniel, followers of Christ often misunderstand what God is doing in their lives. We do not perceive how the mundane and painful matters of our daily lives might be part of His plans to shape us and to make us new. We might harbor the false impression that we are required to obey God's commandments today in order to gain God's favor so that we can enter heaven when we die. We need to remember that God has big plans for His people. He wants us to live in His presence, and therefore He is preparing an eternal home for us.[173] While we endure difficult times, it is comforting to remember that God is preparing a better future. We find peace in knowing that one day God will take away our struggles.

God's plans include making us perfect and holy, just as He is.[174] In order for this to happen, we will need to endure some changes. The thought of these changes, however, can seem very intimidating. How can we hope to be perfect when we hold petty grudges against the people who live down the street, or repeatedly make and break promises? We know that we are far from holy when we acknowledge our enviousness and bitterness towards others or when we struggle with lustful desires. Because we are painfully aware of our own shortcomings, the call to be perfect will cause anxiety. The journey to perfection is a long trip, but it is a journey that Christ's followers will make.

Followers of Christ are being transformed into new creatures. If we do not realize this, we are like Daniel LaRusso, wondering when the difficult and trying times of our chores will be finished so we can start enjoying the eternal inheritance God has promised.

The journey God has planned is more than a trip from this world to heaven. That is only a change of location. God has a plan to change us, which means He is going to transform our hearts.[175] We are in the process of being changed from sinful to sinless.

The Intention to Transform

After God rescued the people of Israel from Egypt, He gave them instruction for living in His presence. These instructions made it clear that God was perfect and holy, and that the only way the people of Israel could be in His presence was if they were transformed in some way.

In the book Leviticus, three categories become clear: holy, clean, and unclean.[176] God is holy. His people must be clean in order to enter His presence, but their hearts are corrupt, and live in a world that constantly makes them unclean. God does not tolerate contact with any uncleanness, so He prescribed various ways in which His people could be cleansed. God introduced a system of cleansing that included sacrifices, ritual washings, and dietary restrictions. The cleanliness He required demanded the keeping of His commands as well as the avoidance of anything that would cause uncleanness.

In order to maintain cleanliness, God's people had to develop the practice of consecration. Consecrate means to set aside for God's purpose. God consecrated the temple, setting it aside as a place where His people could meet with Him. He also consecrated the entire tribe of Levites, setting the Levites aside to remind the people of God's presence and instruction. The Sabbath was a day that was consecrated; set aside from normal weekly activities in order to worship God. If people wanted to make sacrifices, God required them to consecrate themselves, or refrain from activities which would make them unclean.

God's call to be clean was the beginning of His work to transform His people. They were not yet able to be perfect nor holy, but they could be in His presence if they were clean. Cleanliness, however, was not the goal. The goal was to become holy.[177] God's command to His people to be holy demonstrates that God's plan was larger than moving His people from Egypt to Canaan. He was going to transform them into a holy nation.

The New Testament continues the concept of transformation. In his second letter to the Corinthians, Paul explains that followers of Christ "are being transformed into His likeness."[178] The Greek word used in this text is the root of the English word metamorphosis. Metamorphosis is a gradual process of change in which the original object emerges into something that is almost unrecognizable from the original. We often use the word to describe what happens to a caterpillar inside a cocoon. It is transformed from something ugly and slow-moving into something with beautiful wings that flies gracefully through the air. Similarly, followers of Christ are being transformed. We are going through a metamorphosis, moving from the ugliness and death of sin to the beauty, life, and likeness of Christ.

God's laws are not intended merely to make us nice people.[179] They serve as a guide, leading us to become new creatures in Christ Jesus. If we think following Christ is an admirable exercise because it makes us more tolerable to others, we misunderstand God's intentions for us. Submitting to Christ in obedience can make us nicer, more tolerable people, but God's intention is not limited to making us nicer. He intends to make us perfect. The change may come gradually, but in the end, it will render us almost unrecognizable. Like the caterpillar in the cocoon, we are in that process right now, if we are following Christ. Because He is directing the process, we should not fear that we are progressing too slowly. We will be made perfect; our responsibility is to follow Christ faithfully.

Apprentice Followers

If you want to pursue a career, you will likely have to spend some time learning while you are on the job. We acknowledge that people need time to learn new skills, and we expect people to develop those skills as they practice their professions. Law students serve as interns in a lawyer's office before they are fully qualified to practice law. A new bricklayer serves an apprenticeship before he receives the full pay of someone with experience. Student teachers are college students who plan to be teachers but are required to gain some experience in another teacher's classroom before receiving their full credentials.

When I was studying to become a pastor, I was blessed to serve a church in which people often lovingly tolerated my sermons. They understood that even though the church considered me capable of leading worship services, I was not yet an ordained minister. They encouraged me and advised me as I learned through practice.

Followers of Christ walk down similar path in the process of their transformation. Like inexperienced professionals, we awkwardly struggle to become more like Christ. By God's grace, we learn and mature as we go through this process, gradually gaining valuable experience as we follow Him.

The New Testament demonstrates the way in which members of the early church treated new followers of Christ. They did not expect new followers to be fully developed in their walk, and they gently encouraged them to practice their faith as they began to follow Christ.

Acts 15 tells of a controversy that developed between Christian leaders who believed that new believers had to be circumcised, and other Christian leaders who believed that circumcision was not necessary for the new converts. After debating, the leaders decided to send a letter of simple instructions to new Christians, telling them to avoid sexual immorality and also to refrain from eating blood, the meat of strangled animals, and food that was sacrificed to idols.

That was not a burdensome list of requirements! The new Gentile Christians had to control what they ate, and avoid sexual sins. Nowhere did the letter mention circumcision or go into great detail about the laws of cleanliness, or deal with the extensive Jewish dietary restrictions. The letter did not even fully expound on the Ten Commandments. The goal of the church leaders was to give new believers instructions that challenged them to walk faithfully with Christ. Their instructions were fitting and reasonable for new believers, but they also demonstrated that those who desired to follow Christ required a new way of living.

The reason James gave for recommending this limited list of requirements was that the law which Moses gave had been preached and read in the synagogues on every Sabbath.[180] James said that the Jewish people who had become followers of Christ already had a solid foundation of teaching from scripture. For thousands of years the Jewish people had lived in God's presence. The new Gentile believers, however, required slow nurture, because they lacked the benefit of this history. Thus, the early church demonstrated followers of Christ were not expected to be perfect, but that they were expected to cooperate in the process of transformation.

The new believers were challenged to change their lives to follow Christ, without being burdened with the intricacies of Jewish law. They received opportunities to grow in their walk with Christ without the fear of condemnation because they were not yet perfect. Still, as apprentices and followers they had significant work to do.

Followers in Training

All followers of Christ are experiencing an apprenticeship of sorts. We are in training to be perfect, but we are not perfect yet. Many followers of Christ believe they can be perfect if they only try harder. Following Christ does require effort, but no amount of effort will perfect us instantly. We need a long process of training to grow in Christ.

Following Christ can seem like an intimidating concept. How can I follow or imitate Christ when I am corrupt? I can try to be patient, but eventually I will lose my temper. I can try to treat others with kindness, but sooner or later I will act with rudeness. I try to demonstrate servant-like thoughtfulness towards others, but I always seem to fall back into my pattern of selfishness. No matter how hard I try, I am not able to be like Jesus. He was perfect, but I am stained by sin.

Following Jesus is not a result of focused effort. Rather, it is a process of focusing on Him and obeying His regimen for growth.

In Paul's New Testament letters, he uses the image of training to describe how Christians should strive to grow in Christ.

> "Everyone who competes in the games goes into strict training. They do it to get a crown that will not last, but we do it to get a crown that will last forever."[181]

> "Train yourself to be godly. For physical training is of some value, but godliness has value for all things, holding promise both for the present life and the life to come."[182]

"All scripture is God-breathed and is useful for teaching, rebuking, correcting and training in righteousness, so that the man of God may be thoroughly equipped for every good work."[183]

Training does not produce instantaneous change; it brings transformation over a period of time. Therefore, training requires continual effort and perseverance. Imagine reading in a health magazine that people who are flexible enjoy wonderful health benefits. You decide that flexibility is something you should strive for, and since it seems to require less effort than lifting weights or running, you will try it. If your idea of stretching is bending over to tie your shoe, tomorrow would not be a good day for you to try to do the splits. Your chance of success will be very low, and the possibility of injury could be very high. You will want to start slowly. Tomorrow you will try to touch your toes. The next day you will add other stretching exercises. You will probably want to spend 15-30 minutes stretching every day. Slowly, this will loosen your muscles, and you will notice change. The splits might be a possibility in the distant future, but for now you will focus on training.

Striving for perfection is like training to do the splits. No amount of instant effort will be sufficient to bring about the changes necessary to make us perfect. Instead, we train, persevering as we follow Christ, and working steadily to develop new habits and routines that will enhance our walk with Him. We try to imagine how He would want us to treat our annoying neighbor. We walk with Him in prayer, asking for guidance and wisdom. We live a life of disciplined following.

Acquiring discipline often demands we repeat the same movements over and over. When Daniel LaRusso wanted to learn karate, he had to repeat the motions of painting up and down, and he had to sand the wooden floors and wax the cars in a large circular pattern. Though repeating these motions frustrated Daniel, they equipped him for a future in karate.

We long to develop natural movements of turning to Christ. We train so that our instinctive reaction will be to seek God's will in times of trouble, to praise Him in times of success, to intercede for others in their hour of need, and to act with wisdom and decisiveness in moments of crisis. These natural movements of prayer, praise, seeking guidance, and obedience do not happen instantly, but only through training.

Training the Mind

How do we train? How do we gradually nudge our hearts into a natural response of turning to God? How do we develop new habits and routines? Transformation is linked to the renewing of our minds.[184] Part of this mind-renewal involves acquiring knowledge, because our minds are transformed as we learn more about God. When we hear the stories of what God has done for His people, we come to realize that we are following an infinitely powerful and incredibly caring Savior. This realization renews our mind by bringing comfort and reassurance. Our minds are also transformed when we study God's commands and strive to apply them to our lives.

Though experiencing transformation includes obtaining knowledge about God, the renewing of our minds is not limited to gaining information. Renewing of our minds also involves the focus of our minds. Our minds are renewed as we turn to Christ in prayer and by being reminded that He is always with us. Philip Yancey talks about "conscious remembering" as a method of training.[185] He suggests setting our watches to chime hourly as a reminder that we should consider what God has done during the past hour. When we intentionally set aside time to remember God, we are working to renew our mind's focus on Him.

The Bible tells us to "pray continually."[186] When I was younger, I thought this was an unrealistic request. How could I fold my hands, close my eyes and pray when my dad wanted me to mow the lawn? It sounded like a nice ideal, but it was just not realistic. I have now come to understand that prayer is not a formal act that requires a bowed head, folded hands, and closed eyes. It is a turning of your thoughts and attention to God. Brother Lawrence, a monastic who lived in the seventeenth century, once advised a fellow Christian to pray in the following manner:

> "If you…devote yourself entirely to praying to God, you will have accomplished a great feat. He does not ask much of us, merely a thought of Him from time to time, a little act of adoration, sometimes to ask for His grace, sometimes to offer Him your sufferings, at other times to thank Him for the graces, past and present, He has bestowed on you, in the midst of your troubles to take solace in him as often as your can. Lift up your heart to Him during your meals and in company; the least little remembrance will always be most pleasing to Him.
>
> It is not necessary to be always in church to be with God, we can make a private chapel of our heart where we can retire from time to time to commune with Him…
>
> Become accustomed then little by little to adore Him in this way: demand of Him His grace; offer Him your heart from time to time during the day in the midst of your work, at every moment if you can; do not burden yourself with rules or particular devotions but act with faith, with love, and with humility."

When I thought of prayer as a formal ritual, I did not think it possible to pray without ceasing, but when I understand that prayer is a turning of our thoughts and minds to God, I realize that it is possible to pray without ceasing. I can live in God's presence by paying attention to the fact that He is always present. Therefore, I can pray while I am driving to and from work, or when I see someone as I am walking down the street, I can turn my mind to God and pray for that person. Just as I was writing this paragraph, I saw my sons playing with our neighbor boys, and I thanked God for good neighbors and the joys of childhood.

Prayer is turning our minds to God. It is one way in which we experience training to be more like Christ. Jesus repeatedly sought solitude so that He could be alone with His Father in prayer. Imitating

His life of prayer slowly reorients our minds to an awareness of God's presence in all of our situations.

Works in Progress

Slow processes can be frustrating, especially when we are eager to meet a goal. I remember going to my grandma's house as a child. Grandma was a wonderful cook. Every time we went there for Sunday dinner, we had roast with mashed potatoes and gravy. She always prepared fresh corn or beans as well as a selection of salads and breads. As the aroma of the meal filled the house and the dinner hour approached, I grew impatient. Minutes went by, and I became frustrated with Grandma's slow process of preparation. Similarly, Christians may grow frustrated with the process of transformation. It takes a long time. In fact, sometimes we wonder whether we are making any progress at all.

When we come to know Christ or begin to take our faith seriously, we can experience a wonderful time of spiritual growth. We understand that we need to be changed, and we make a concerted effort to live differently. We believe that God is working and take delight in the renewing of our minds as we seek Him in prayer. We willingly imitate Christ and submit to Him in obedience. Slowly, however, our enthusiasm fades. Even though we continue to train our minds through spiritual disciplines as we follow Christ, the initial sense of progress seems to dwindle. We wonder whether we are actually moving on this journey to be transformed.

We must remember that the journey from being lost in sin to being perfected in Christ is a long one that will not be completed until Christ returns. Long journeys often have stretches during which progress seems minimal. When my family takes a road trip, everyone is enthusiastic at the beginning. We are glad that the packing is completed, and we feel a sense of progress as the van begins to accelerate down the highway. The journey usually begins with dreamy-eyed hopes of the fun that our destination will bring. Soon, however, the excitement of our road trip fades, and traveling in the van becomes rather boring. Our children start asking the repeated question that drives me crazy, "Are we there yet?" We wonder if we are making any progress. I know the van is moving at 70 miles per hour, but it doesn't feel as if we are getting anywhere.

When I reach this point in the journey, I can no longer trust my senses. Because my enthusiasm has faded, I have to look to trust other signals. Even though the scenery of cornfields seems unending, I know that we are moving when I look at the speedometer. If I have been following the directions and keeping the van between the lines on the road, I can be relatively confident that we are moving in the right direction. I trust that the trip is still moving forward, even though my enthusiasm has faded.

In our journey to become like Christ, we will experience moments, perhaps even long periods of time, when it seems as if we are making little or no progress. We may not feel the excitement that we felt early in the trip as the hope of our eternal destiny get pushed aside by the tasks of the day. The scenery of prayer, worship, service, and training may become redundant, and we might begin to think that we are stuck in a formalistic rut.

When we reach this point in the journey, we should look for other signs of progress. Our feelings of growth are not always good indicators of our progress as we follow Christ. We would do well to answer questions like the following: Do we believe that Jesus is worth following? Do we trust Christ has taken care of our deepest needs? Are we striving to follow God's commands? Do we have an assurance that God is caring for us? If we can honestly say yes to these questions, we are likely moving forward on our spiritual trip even though we cannot feel the progress.

We should also, however, be open to the possibility that we have stopped training. Perhaps we are no longer making an effort to focus our minds on Christ and His grace. Perhaps we are beginning to slow down on the journey because we are slowly hardening our hearts. If our loss of enthusiasm is a result of rebellion or loss of focus, we should turn to God in prayer and ask Him to help us in our training. We should ask Him to help us develop the disciplines to seek Him continually.

God's transforming process may be slow and imperceptible, but He is working. As we train to become more like Christ, we must avoid the false assumption that progress is a direct result of our efforts. Remember, all of this training is simply putting up our sails to catch the moving power of God's wind, the Holy Spirit. The Holy Spirit moves us according to His desires;[187] we cannot induce spiritual growth through our own efforts. Even though we may practice and train, our best efforts do nothing more than put us in a position to cooperate with the Holy Spirit's power to change us.

We can be assured that God is moving forward with His plans to transform us. We may not think progress is being made, but neither did Daniel LaRusso. Our job is not to make progress, but simply to continue following wherever Christ would lead.

Observable Progress

Even though we will be transformed slowly, we should expect to see some progress in our walk with God. We might begin to share our faith with confidence or feel comfortable serving within a church. Perhaps we will notice progress as we develop the habit prayer, or we might notice that our desires have changed from pleasing self to pleasing God.

The New Testament writers expected noticeable progress in the journey of being transformed. In the letter to the Corinthian Christians, Paul seems frustrated because the followers of Christ are still separated by petty jealousies and silly debates. He writes to them explaining that he expected more progress in their walk with Christ.[188]

The goal of this chapter so far has been to show that perfection, or sanctification, is a long and gradual process. Because it is important for followers of Christ to observe change as they grow, we must also consider noticeable change.

If we are following Christ, we should notice changes as a result of looking to Him. If we are trying to imitate Him and training our minds to consciously remember Him, we will be changed. We may notice a greater sense of peace that frames our perspective of life, or find it easier to forgive others, realizing that we have been forgiven. We might discover that we do not struggle with the same temptations that formerly plagued our lives. We might have a greater awareness of the joys in our lives or the beauty of what God has done in this world.

Because following Christ will make us new, we should notice changes when we follow Him. For some people following Christ will mean radical changes in a very short period of time. For example, prior to his conversion, Saint Augustine had pursued secular career. He had a child with a woman he never married, and later sought to marry another woman, who, he hoped, would advance his stature. He accepted many strange and unique philosophical teachings, but rejected the authority of Christ. After God converted him, Augustine no longer sought a wife, and he also gave up his ambition for success.[189] His life changed drastically from that point. His conversion began a process of transformation from a secular philosopher who ran from God into one of the most revered church leaders since the completion of the New Testament. Clearly, God made noticeable changes in his life.

God's changes may come slowly, and He may not make the changes we desire. Paul prayed repeatedly that God would remove a "thorn,"[190] but God never did. Even though God refused that request, we would agree that God did bring about noticeable transformation in Paul's life. Paul had been transformed from an enemy of Christ's followers[191] to a leader in Christ's church.[192]

Like Paul, we should not expect that God will change us in every way we desire, at least not immediately. We will still struggle with weakness and temptation, but God is making progress in the lives of His followers. He does bring His peace and contentment to those who follow Him. He will make sure that our efforts for His Kingdom will not return empty.[193]

When God began His work in you, you were dead in sin. He has already granted you new life. His Holy Spirit is making progress in the job to sanctify you. One day, that job will be completed.

Restored to Original Condition

In my early life, I believed the goal of Christians was to go to heaven when they die, a noble and joyful goal, but incomplete. God desires to do more than change our location; He wants to change the condition of our hearts, so that we can be in His presence. The New Testament describes Christ's union with His followers in a number of ways: Christ is in us, we are in Christ, and we are with Christ.[194] This kind of unity with God is reminiscent of the fellowship Adam and Eve enjoyed with God in the Garden of Eden. God is working to restore that original goal of creation.

When God made Adam, he was without sin, able to be in His presence. Adam was created in His image, reflecting His glory. Sin, however, caused a separation from God; it damaged the way we reflect God's glory. In His love, God is now working to restore the union we had with Him at the time of creation. His plan includes taking us to heaven when we die, but He also gives us the privilege of being in His presence right now. We know He is present when He hears our prayers, when we gather in His name,[195] and when He guides us and comforts us. This unity requires a transformed heart.

God is working to restore the condition of the human heart. One day, it will no longer be corrupted by sin. One day we will have no shame in His presence, because we will be restored to His image, just as He intended.

Questions for discussion/reflection:
What does it mean to be holy?

Does God expect too much of us when He calls us to be holy? Why or why not?

Name some ways we can renew our minds in order to be transformed.

Why is it difficult to observe progress as Christ transforms us?

Chapter 9
Blending into the Crowd

"Follow the Leader" is not much fun when you play it by yourself. It is intended to be a group game. I love to see children gathered together, often in long lines, attempting to imitate the leader of the pack. Sometimes, the line is so long that the people in back cannot possibly imitate the leader. Instead, they simply imitate the people in front of them. If one child makes a mistake, many might be prone to copy that mistake. If one child falls down, those who were following him might learn from his mistake and avoid the accident.

As we follow Christ, we are not following alone. In the world today, there are millions who gather together every Sunday to worship Jesus. We are following with many people who are living today. Furthermore, we often find ourselves like children in the back of a long line as they play "follow the leader." We realize that much of what we know about Jesus is what other followers of Christ have passed down to us. Paul told Corinthian Christians to "imitate me."[196] The author of Hebrews instructed his readers to imitate the faith of other people.[197] We are to imitate people who imitate Christ. As we do this, we still acknowledge that there is One Leader who is setting the pace. We are still worshipping Him, but we learn and benefit from our fellow followers.

In the preceding chapters, I have been describing the implications of being a follower of Christ. I have been speaking primarily in individual terms. Each of us struggles with our sinful nature. We each are called to imitate Christ. Each one of Christ's followers is experiencing His transforming power.

We do not follow Christ alone. God has blessed us with a

community of followers who might have little in common outside the desire to follow Him.

It's A Team Effort

Jesus told His disciples that those who have faith in Him will do even greater thing than He did.[198] To many followers of Christ, this seems unlikely. Jesus performed amazing miracles. He calmed storms, healed diseases, cast out demons, and raised people from the dead. How can His followers do things that are even greater?

In the book of Acts, we see what Jesus was talking about. Jesus' disciples continued His work. They healed and proclaimed the good news of Jesus' Kingdom. They stood boldly before hostile crowds and affirmed their faith in Christ, even in the face of threats upon their lives. Jesus did incredible things through them.

In Acts, the number of Jesus' followers grew well beyond what they were at any point during Jesus' earthly ministry. Prior to His crucifixion, Jesus was a popular figure. After He ascended into heaven, His followers extended to the ends of known world. Jesus' used His disciples to make His ministry greater than it ever was during His life. His words were true. The disciples did do even greater things.

Following His ascension, Jesus' disciples established the body of believers, the church. In this church, there were many leaders, but there was only one Lord, Jesus Christ. One of the benefits of using so many people to establish His church was that Christ's followers started to learn that Jesus was permanently with them, even though He had ascended into heaven. They learned that even though there were many leaders that were used by God, none of them were replacements for Jesus. He is the One we follow.

When children are growing, one of the lessons they need to learn is object permanence.[199] They do not naturally understand that their parents still exist when they are not in their physical proximity. They need to be in Mom and Dad's presence to know that Mom and Dad are still alive. The early church may have struggled with this concept of object permanence regarding Jesus. They could no longer see Him, walk with Him, nor eat with Him. It might have been hard for them to believe that He was still with them in any way. Jesus had taught His disciples that He would send His Holy Spirit after His ascension.[200] He assured them that they would not be left alone. Once He ascended, the disciples and all who had come to follow Him needed to experience that reality.

When a child develops normally, she learns through experience that Mom and Dad are real and living, even when they are not within visual range. Christ's early church learned to be assured that Jesus was with them, even though they could not see Him. As the leaders of their group (who were followers of Christ) performed miracles, proclaimed the good news, and welcomed new people into their fellowship, Christ's followers learned that He indeed was still with them.

I doubt this would have happened if Jesus had selected a single successor. If Peter or John or James had been named the sole leader, it could have seemed as though that individual was now the leader of a continuing movement. The need for Jesus would have been minimized, because it would have appeared that one of the disciples had now become the great rabbi of a movement that Jesus had started.

In the United States of America, we hold the memory of George Washington in high regard. He was the first president of our nation. He set a great example for future presidents. However, we do not hold on to any illusions that he is still mysteriously at work in our nation today. We have selected new presidents throughout history, who have filled the office originally held by Washington. He was a great leader, but he has been replaced.

By using a group of people to continue His work, Jesus did not leave room for the impression that He was being replaced.[201] His followers were given the assignment to make more disciples for Him,[202] not for themselves. He was, and still is the Leader. His followers cooperate to help each other follow Him

Jesus is still at work today. He continues to build His church by the work of His Holy Spirit. He still raises leaders to take care of His flock.[203] Although we may look for new leaders in our churches when the former leaders step down, we are looking for people who will point us to the same Savior who has always been proclaimed in His church.

This team concept should bring us great comfort. Maybe you are a person who believes that if you want something done right, you have to do it yourself. Perhaps you feel the burden of responsibility whenever you see something going awry. You believe that you should fix anything that might not be right. In short, you want to save the world.

It is a noble desire to want to save the world. The bad news is, you are not capable. You do not have the time, the energy, or the resources to respond to every need around you. In fact, if you try to respond to every need around you, you will end up neglecting the most significant priorities in your life.

Occasionally, I need to be reassured that my job is not to fix the world, but to follow Christ. I can take comfort following Christ, because I know that He sees all the needs of the world. He knows which needs I should respond to, and which needs I should allow others to respond to. I do not have to save the world, because that is Christ's work. I have to follow where He leads and submit to his instruction. The good news is that Christ has many followers. I may not be able to fix a particular problem, but Christ can easily raise someone who can.

If you do struggle with a "save the world" mentality, if you feel the burden of every need you see, be assured that Christ sees those needs too. He will lead you where He wants you to serve, so listen carefully. And if His leading takes you away from a problem you would like to fix, trust that He will provide what is needed. He has many people He can call.

The Joy of Community

After Elijah had tremendous success revealing the power of God on Mount Carmel,[204] he was forced to run for his life. Even though he had been used in tremendous ways by God, he was ready to die. He was tired of feeling all alone in his desire to serve God.[205] One of his primary complaints was that he felt isolated.

One of the incredible things about 1 Kings 19 is that God does not in any way rebuke Elijah for feeling all alone. Instead, God responds lovingly to Elijah and shows him that there were others who were going to join Elijah in God's service. Elijah was called from his hiding to anoint two kings and a new prophet. Immediately following that incident there are other prophets mentioned in 1 Kings. As readers, we get to see that Elijah was really never alone in his zeal to serve God.

Feeling isolated can be devastating to a person's faith. We need others around us to encourage us and sustain us in our walk with God. God had a great plan in mind when He began the New Testament church. He created a fellowship of believers. The ongoing work of Jesus Christ was not left in the hands of any single person. It was left for all of His followers to share.

The joy of community is a tremendously precious gift. In the book of Acts, there is a wonderful description of the fellowship enjoyed by followers of Christ in the early church.[206] They ate together, worshipped together, and shared everything they had with each other. Their fellowship was contagious, and many were added to their number daily.

When I was in high school, I would feel guilty about my attitude towards church. I looked forward to going to church, but I feared it was for the wrong reasons. I wanted to go to church, because that was where I saw my closest friends. I did not mind listening to sermons or attending church education classes, but that was not what I most anticipated about going to church. I wanted to see my friends.

I felt guilty, because I believed that if I truly loved Jesus, I would find sheer joy in attending classes and singing songs and listening to the preaching of His Word. I believed my motives were less than pure.

As I have grown, I have come to understand that the joy and pleasure of friendship and fellowship is one of the blessings God intended for us in His church. Jesus prayed that His followers would be one.[207] He wants us to be united. He wants us to enjoy each other's company. This is one of the gifts He gives us.

There are many ways to worship God. I can pray while I am driving down the road. I can hear a good sermon from dozens of preachers on television throughout the week. I can read books and read the Bible so that I will be edified as I grow in my knowledge of God. None of these, however, stimulates fellowship with other believers. God established His church because He wanted us to meet together.[208]

When my family goes on vacation, I enjoy attending different churches. It is good to see that God's Kingdom work is carried on in many different places. I am pleased to hear various ministers proclaim that Jesus is Lord. I enjoy hearing and singing music that glorifies God. However, it is always good to return home to our church family. There, God has given me the gift of people who know me. People there know about my struggles as a pastor and as a parent. They have prayed for my family members and demonstrated care and kindness toward my children. Because we meet together regularly, there is an intimacy that goes beyond simple fondness for one another. This is a gift God has intended for His people. This is the joy of the fellowship of believers.

Since I am a pastor, people will sometimes ask me if it is sinful to skip Sunday worship services. It seems as though they want to know which reasons are legitimate excuses for missing church. I usually respond by saying something like, "I don't know if it is a sin to skip an opportunity to worship with others, but I know that when we miss gathering together with God's people, we miss an opportunity to be blessed by other followers of Christ." I do not fear condemnation for missing church worship services. I fear that when we neglect to gather with other followers of Christ, we are missing the investment of time that is required to develop close friendships. I fear that we might end up thinking fondly of other believers without experiencing the intimate oneness that Christ desired.

Learning from Others

It is good to have many people pointing you in the same direction.

When I was in elementary school, I struggled in the subject of grammar. I could not memorize the different types of words and punctuation. What was the difference between conjunctions and prepositions? When should I use commas, and when should I use semi-colons? My teachers taught properly, but I struggled to retain their instruction.

FOLLOW THE LEADER

I experienced a watershed moment one Saturday morning when I saw a cartoon music video on television about conjunctions, and how they acted like cars of a train.[209] The short video did not tell me something new, but it helped cement in my mind the instruction I had been receiving from my teacher. It was helpful to have multiple sources teaching and reinforcing the same lessons.

When someone is a member of a church, he has the benefit of many fellow believers pointing him in the same direction; to follow Christ. It may happen in a variety of ways. A minister can preach on Sunday morning. A Sunday School teacher can reiterate those lessons. A Bible Study leader can point out passages that direct how we should live. Small group leaders can demonstrate how God's lessons can be applied to our daily lives. All of these people work together to point a person to follow Christ.

In my church, we baptize infants. When my children were baptized, I made a promise to do all I can to help them become disciples of Jesus. To my delight, at their baptism ceremonies, the congregation made promises to support me in that endeavor. I am not usually an emotional person, but when my son, Isaac, at age 2, came home from Children's Worship singing "Jesus Loves Me" for the first time, I was overwhelmed with gratitude. Someone took that promise, to help me and my wife, seriously. Someone took time out of their week to teach my son a song that reinforces the reality that Jesus loves him. My wife and I take time to teach our children about Christ. One of our most often repeated prayer requests is that they will know how much Christ loves them and that they will have a deep desire to live for Him. It is comforting to know that we are not alone in our prayer requests and efforts. There are other people out there reinforcing the lessons we try to teach, just like the song about conjunctions reinforced what my grammar teacher had taught me.

But it is not merely reinforced in Sunday School. People in the back of church will warmly greet my children and lovingly interact with them. My sons have come to think of their church as I used to think of extended family. They are comfortable being around people from their church. I have no family relationships with people in my church. The only thing that unites us is that we are fellow followers of Jesus Christ, and that is enough for those wonderful people to make promises to reinforce the work of Christ in the lives of my children. I thank God for them.

The Accountability of Community

As iron sharpens iron, so one man sharpens another.[210]

When I was in college, I thought it was important to exercise. You might not believe that if you looked at me today, but I really did. I tried exercising in a number of different ways. I swam. I ran. I did calisthenics. They were all effective exercises. The only problem was, I didn't maintain a disciplined schedule for exercising. My routine was rather hit-or-miss, and I missed a lot more than I hit. Not until my sophomore year did I discover how to maintain a good workout schedule. I found someone who would exercise with me. Steve and I would meet regularly and lift weights together. This was effective because there was someone else holding me accountable. When I wanted to skip lifting and take an afternoon nap, I would remember that Steve was waiting for me. This accountability was good for me because it kept me following a good plan for my health.

God has established a good plan for following Christ. It includes other people holding us accountable. For many followers of Christ, the difficulty following is not that worship is meaningless or prayer is ineffective. The difficulty lies in our tendencies to be lazy in how we pursue Christ. Having other people hold us accountable is a tremendous blessing because it keeps us from succumbing to laziness in our walk with God.

Peer pressure often has negative connotations. Many adolescents feel pressure to be like their peers and engage in activities that are detrimental to their well being. However, peer pressure can have a positive side. When our peers are followers of Jesus, and the pressure they exert is directed to help us remain faithful to Christ, they are helping us grow nearer to Him.

This positive peer pressure does not come in the form of an ultimatum. It comes through gently encouraging and caring for one another. If you look up all the times Paul uses the words "each other" or "one another" in his New Testament letters, you will find a wonderful range of texts that teach us how fellow believers can encourage each other and hold each other accountable.

"Be devoted to one another."[211]
"Live in harmony with one another."[212]
"Let us stop passing judgment on one another."[213]
"Accept one another."[214]
"Greet one another with a holy kiss."[215]
"Serve one another in love."[216]
"Carry each other's burdens."[217]
"Be patient, bearing with one another."[218]
"Be kind and compassionate to one another, forgiving each other, just as in Christ God forgave you."[219]
"Submit to one another out of reverence for Christ."[220]
"Let the word of Christ dwell in your richly as you teach and admonish one another."[221]
"You yourselves have been taught by God to love each other."[222]
"Encourage one another and build each other up."[223]
"Live in peace with each other."[224]

From this instruction we recognize that God desires a high level of intimacy between His people. He desires a kind of intimacy that includes kindness, and a willingness to admonish each other. This kind of community gives us assurance that we are loved and accepted, and calls us to be faithful as we follow Christ. This kind of community demonstrates God's love for us, and calls us to demonstrate God's love to others. We are blessed when we experience this kind of fellowship.

As followers of Christ, we should make an effort to find people we admire, and attempt to imitate them and draw nearer to them. I believe I have had many different mentors who have led me closer to Christ. I never was part of a formal mentorship program, but there have been many people who have blessed me and helped me grow closer to Christ.

Do you have people in your life that you admire? Are there people in your life who treat you the way the New Testament instructs us to treat fellow followers? People with those qualities can be found in Christian churches around the world. But we have to look carefully. Many aspire to be like Christ, but not all have matured in their faith. This may be why the Bible places a special call upon those who have mature faith to teach and instruct younger men and women.[225]

If there are people you admire because of their faith in Christ, try to get to know them better and imitate the characteristics you admire. When I have to make a difficult decision, I often find myself wondering how someone I admire would respond. I am pleased to report that I can often imagine how they would act, and it helps me make better decisions. That is part of the process of iron sharpening iron. God uses us to mold and shape each other.

Unity of Common Goals

When I first started training in Tae Kwon Do, I was struck by the diversity in the class. The students were a mixture of people from varying ethnic backgrounds. People from Asian, European, African, Philippine, and Hispanic descent all worked out at the same time. There were days that I would hear three different languages spoken in class. College graduates would work out with high school dropouts. Police officers, pilots, lawyers, bartenders, photographers, social workers and prison guards would train together. There were people from different religious backgrounds. In fact, the only common interest I could find between these people was a desire to become more proficient in their martial arts training. It might be hard to believe, but this common interest was enough to create a great sense of unity within that class. As students, we would strive together, encourage each other, and learn from one another. We became friends. We learned more about each other. From a diverse group of people, a community was formed around martial arts.

There were a number of factors that worked to unite our class. We all learned from the same teacher. We trained together regularly. We knew that we had a lot of room for improvement. Most notably, we shared a desire to improve. Each one of us wanted to work our way through the various color belts in order to receive the black belt.

I am amazed at how a group of people can be drawn closer together when they share a common goal. This kind of closeness is not unique to martial arts. Many team sports draw people together from different backgrounds, with different gifts, to pursue a common goal. People who have served in the military will often attest to the unity they experienced with their fellow soldiers as they accepted assignments that put them in harm's way.

Followers of Christ experience a unity that is based in the pursuit of common goals. We grow closer to each other as we worship and serve Christ together. We serve the same Lord. Even though we speak many different languages, live on different continents, and have vastly different cultural backgrounds, we experience the unity of being part of God's family when we follow Christ together.

This unity is enhanced when we focus on our common goals. When we strive to bring God honor and glory, barriers of culture and race are shattered. As we realize that all of Christ's followers are striving to imitate Him as they are being transformed, we come to understand that our common goals are much greater than our diversified backgrounds. We are united by our desire to follow the Leader. When following Christ is the focus of our lives, we are welcomed into an intimate family of God's children.

Family Feuds

Sadly, this unity often breaks down. Maybe the previous section about unity within Christ's church sounded a little too idealistic to you. You have seen too many church battles over senseless issues. You see the landscape of denominations in our world, and you notice Christ's followers working tirelessly to differentiate themselves from each other. The unity within God's family is not what it should be.

Before we explore the dynamics of the breakdown between followers of Christ, I want to pause to marvel at the fact that even though the unity between Christians is not what it should be, God works in marvelous ways to unite different people. Christ's followers often come together to advance His kingdom in remarkable ways. There have been countless numbers of Christ's followers who have abandoned their homes and lifestyles to follow Him to different countries. There are many followers of Christ who work tirelessly to learn new languages and study the etiquette of different cultures for the purpose of bringing the good news of Jesus Christ to other people. Because of a desire to be faithful to Jesus, there are followers of Christ from different racial and economic backgrounds who make an intentional effort to grow closer to each other to honor their Lord.

Despite these hopeful signs, we still must admit that the unity between Christ's followers is often subjected to petty rivalries and divisions. Far too often, followers of Christ accentuate their differences, rather than focusing on the common goals of growing in Christ and glorifying Him. That old sinful nature with our guilt and corruption rears its ugly head, and the unity within Christ's body suffers.

Some of this division is a result of honest disagreements. Because we are stained by sin, we often misunderstand each other, or disagree over how we should understand God's word. I am a pastor in a church where children of believers are baptized. There are some churches that teach only believers should be baptized. I have witnessed and participated in many debates over the issue of infant baptism. Even though I believe my church is correct in its interpretation of God's word, I do not believe that those who disagree are being unfaithful to God simply because they disagree with me. Even if we approach each other with compassion and understanding, it is difficult to maintain unity in the face of these kinds of debates. If we are passionate about following Christ, and I hope we are, then our disagreements over how we understand God's word will quickly become issues that can cause division.

Have you ever noticed that family disagreements are often the most hostile? Brothers and sisters will often fight with each other much more ferociously than neighbors or casual acquaintances. It seems as though there must be some kind of common ground for us to even believe there is something worth fighting for.

Disagreements between Christ's followers are family disagreements. The fact that we disagree does not necessarily indicate a lack of love for each other. Sometimes, we disagree because we love each other, and we worry that our fellow followers may go astray.

There are other divisions that are more sinister. Often, we find that we are separated from one another because we have lost the focus of following Christ. We might desire our personal gratification more than Christ's glory. We are often quick to notice the speck of dust in our brother's eye while ignoring our own vision problems.[226] We allow the desire to "win a debate" overshadow our desire to follow Christ.

Perhaps you love Christ, but you get terribly annoyed by His other followers. Part of the process of being made new involves learning to work with our fellow followers of Christ. Christ loves each one of us, and He prayed that we would be united.[227]

Christ's followers are not a perfect bunch. But amazingly, Christ has continued to work through this imperfect group for centuries. As we follow our Leader, we notice the mistakes that we all make. We notice how our mistakes affect each other. Yet we move forward with the confidence that our Leader will somehow complete the process He has begun in each one of us.

A Long Line of Predecessors

Jesus used an unlikely group of followers to begin an incredible movement. Since Christ has returned to heaven, powerful nations have risen and fallen. Kings have been born and died. People have risen to positions of notoriety, only to be forgotten by their successors. Yet the good news of Jesus Christ continues to be proclaimed. The Bible continues to be translated into different languages. People from varying nations and races are drawn together and united in their desire to follow Him.

Christians today are members of a long line of followers. As we follow Christ we learn from those who are following with us today, as well as those who have gone before us. Like children playing "follow the leader," we can gain great insights from those followers who have gone before us. We can learn from the ways God successfully used them, and we can learn from their shortcomings.

In the next chapter, we are going to begin a new phase in this book. We are going to look at some of Christ's first followers. We are going to learn from the way God worked in the lives of Peter, John, Thomas, and others. We will take note of Christ's expectations for those followers. We will see that God was able to use them despite their shortcomings. We may learn about dangers that we should avoid. Members of the early New Testament Church are our fellow followers. We want to imitate them as they imitated Christ, and we want to be reassured that God can use us in powerful ways, as He used that unlikely group.

Questions for discussion/reflection:
Who are some people you admire for their faith in Christ? How have you tried to imitate them?

How can the perspective of following Christ keep us from being consumed by the troubles in the world?

Why is it important to worship with other believers regularly?

How do you see Christians practice accountability in their walk with God? How should you practice accountability?

How should Christians handle "feuds" within the church?

Chapter 10
Peter: Bold and Prone to Stumble

I thank God for Peter.

Whenever I read stories of Peter, I feel like I am looking in a mirror. He is prone to put his foot in his mouth. He is bold, and sometimes oversteps his authority. He can look brilliant one moment, and foolish the next. I feel a kinship with Peter, because I see my own shortcomings; whenever I experience a momentary triumph, it is frequently followed by a terrible lapse in judgment.

Peter was the only disciple who walked on water.[228] He had the chutzpah to request that Christ let him experience this miraculous feat, and his request was granted. Asking Christ for permission to walk on water was a sign of great faith, but it was followed by a moment of doubt. Peter's temporary triumph became a moment of embarrassment.

Peter professed that he would never forsake Christ, even if it meant he had to die.[229] It was a touching testimony of dedication. However, Peter was not able to live up to his intentions. Less than 24 hours later, he denied knowing Christ.

Peter was impulsive. He often became too bold, taking matters into his own hands when he should have stepped aside. When Jesus explained that He would suffer and die, Peter became presumptuous and rebuked Jesus for His talk about suffering. To that, Jesus responded by saying, "Get behind me, Satan."[230] On another occasion, Peter drew his sword in order to protect his Lord. Again, Jesus had to rebuke Peter for interfering with His Father's plans.[231]

Peter was able to see Jesus' glory, but could not accept His suffering.[232] When Jesus' glory was revealed during His transfiguration, Peter wanted to stay right there.[233] But when Jesus spoke of suffering, Peter was unable to submit.

I am thankful for Peter, because I see my own tendency to try to take matters into my own hands when things are not going the way I want them to. I am prone to stumble and say the wrong thing. Despite my best intentions, I allow my instincts to guide me when I should submit to my Lord.

I am hopeful when I read accounts of Peter, because despite his weaknesses, Jesus was able to use him. Peter may have been a bold disciple who was prone to act impulsively, but he was the one used by God to preach on the first Pentecost Sunday.[234] On that day, about 3,000 people became followers of Christ.

I am encouraged by Peter, because in him I can see that God uses imperfect people to accomplish incredible feats. As a follower of Christ who is prone to stumble, I am reassured that God can use even me, with all of my flaws, when I see the powerful ways He used Peter.

The Testimony

When Jesus asked His disciples about His identity, Peter was the disciple to correctly identify Him as the Christ who had been promised in the Old Testament.[235] This is a pivotal moment in Peter's life. After this testimony, Jesus said that He would build His church on this rock.[236] This testimony was followed by Christ declaring that Peter was given authority in His kingdom to bind and loose.

God did go on to use Peter and his confession of Christ in powerful ways. Many Biblical scholars believe that Peter's testimony was crucial in the development of the first three gospels, Matthew, Mark, and Luke.

The author of the Gospel of Mark is believed to have been one of Peter's assistants as he worked to spread the good news of Jesus. If this is true, then Mark's account of Jesus is a reflection of Peter's preaching and teaching. Furthermore, scholars generally agree that Matthew and Luke both used Mark as a key source in writing their accounts of Jesus' life. If scholars are correct in their theories about the development of the gospel accounts, then Peter's testimony truly was a rock on which

Christ's church has been built.

Through Peter's testimony, we see the ideas of following and imitating being exercised. Peter served our Lord as he proclaimed the good news of Jesus Christ. Mark imitated Peter in proclaiming that good news. Luke and Matthew then imitated Mark. Christ's good news was advanced as His followers learned from each other, and Peter played a significant role in that process. Christ used Him as a leader in His church.

Lessons for Leaders

Many books have been written on the subject of leadership. Apparently, many people wish to acquire the skills and charisma to compel other people to follow them. We live in a time when leaders are revered. Organizations are looking for people with leadership skills. Churches want pastors who will be effective leaders.

In our human idea of wisdom, most of us would not choose the well known leaders in the Bible to lead our churches. Many of the leaders in the Old and New Testaments had flaws that would be difficult to overlook. We would not like David, because he was known to have a weakness regarding the opposite sex.[237] Samson would be overlooked because of his rebellious streak.[238] We would reject Paul, because he was known to preach too long.[239] Joseph would not be approved, because he was a dreamer who could not even get along with his own family.[240] We would not want to recommend Elisha because he did not always show respect to leaders.[241] Moses would have to be passed over because he was known to lose his temper in stressful situations.[242] However, in our human wisdom, we might opt for someone who had demonstrated concern for the poor and was known to be good with money; someone like Judas Iscariot.[243]

God has different priorities when He chooses leaders for His church. Throughout the Bible, we find God selecting unlikely people to use for incredible tasks. Humans look for leaders with charisma who instill a sense of confidence. Many of the leaders God chose were not prime candidates for leadership by human standards. But God was able to use them to fulfill His purposes.

Peter does seem to demonstrate qualities that we look for in our leaders. He is bold enough to ask Christ if he can walk on water. He is not afraid to speak on behalf of the group. He seems more than willing to speak his mind. Peter is very gifted to be a leader, but giftedness is not sufficient for leaders in Christ's church. We must be submissive to Christ. This is particularly difficult for people with natural leadership skills, because leaders want to take charge; they do not want to submit to the will of another. Peter struggled as he was shaped by Christ because he had to learn to submit to Christ, especially when Christ spoke of His intention to suffer.

Leaders in Christ's church must first realize that they are followers. When we focus on leadership, it becomes very easy to succumb to the temptation to be consumed with leadership skills and abilities. We emphasize the mechanics of motivating people. We force ourselves to be bold in our presentation.

Leadership can become a weakness when we focus on leadership techniques, and allow our eyes to wander from Christ. Leaders in God's family must focus on Christ and welcome their fellow followers to join them in their journey.

Studying leadership techniques can be helpful, but we must remember that in Christ's church, we are all followers of the One true Leader. Leaders in the church must remember that their first calling is to be a follower. As they follow, they learn that leadership in Christ's church requires humility and a willingness to serve.[244]

The Need for Submission

Before Peter could be an effective leader, he had to become a submissive follower. Undoubtedly, Peter had leadership skills. He was bold and able to get people to listen to him. He was not afraid to say what was on his mind. He seemed to be loyal and optimistic about the future.

God was able to use Peter's gifts, but first, Peter had to learn to submit to his Master. When we are followers of Christ, we are committed to Jesus as a person. We must also be committed to Christ's plans. We must submit our desires to Him.

Peter was personally committed to Christ. He correctly identified

Him. He recognized Jesus' power. He understood that Jesus was truly from God. However, Peter was less enthusiastic than about following Jesus' plans. He did not like the idea of Jesus suffering. He went to great lengths to voice His disapproval.

When Jesus first revealed His plan to suffer and die, Peter objected, defying His master and saying, "This will never happen to you."[245] When Jesus' glory was revealed on the mountain, Peter suggested they stay there, avoiding the dangers and suffering Christ had foretold.[246] Even when Jesus was captured in the garden before His trial, Peter would not submit to Christ's plan to suffer. He took up his sword against the Roman soldiers.[247] Peter may have intended to be loyal to his Lord, but His actions demonstrated that He was unwilling to submit.

You may wonder about Peter's loyalty. After all, Peter denied knowing Jesus during the trial that led to His crucifixion. How can we call Peter loyal? It is true that Peter was weak, and he did deny Jesus. But it does not appear that Peter intended to be disloyal.

Before Jesus was arrested, Peter had declared his loyalty.[248] He boldly proclaimed that even if all others fell away from Jesus, he never would. There is no reason to believe that Peter was intentionally lying to Jesus in this moment. His actions later proved that he was sincere. He was willing to take up the sword for Jesus. He was willing to follow Jesus into the courtyard during the trial. However, Peter was not as strong as he had thought. He believed that he would always be faithful to Jesus. But when push came to shove, he backed down. When asked if he was one of Jesus' followers, he lied and swore and claimed he had never met the man.[249]

Peter's denial may not have been intentional betrayal, but it revealed his weakness. Before his denial, Peter may have thought he was loyal to Christ. He may have believed his plans were better than Jesus' plans. But in the moment he realized his own treachery, Peter knew that he could no longer follow his own way.

Followers of Christ must be committed to Christ and willing to follow His plans. We must avoid the pitfall of believing that we can be committed to the person of Christ while negotiating over His will for our lives. Christ wants our loyalty, but He tells us that a relationship with Him obligates us to submit in obedience.[250]

Peter learned a great deal about himself and about Christ on the night of Christ's arrest. He learned that Christ knew him better than he knew himself. He believed that he would remain loyal to Christ, even to death. Christ knew Peter would deny Him. When we follow Christ, we are following One who knows us better than we know ourselves. He knows our weaknesses. He knows our shortcomings. He even knows the illusions we have about ourselves. Even though Peter may have been sincere in his desire to be loyal, he was not strong enough to honor that intention.

Peter also learned that he had to submit to Christ's plans. He was humbled on the night of Jesus' arrest. After recognizing his treachery, Peter went out and wept bitterly.

Reinstated

In each of the gospels that are believed to be based on Peter's testimony, we never read of Jesus and Peter speaking privately after Peter's denials. In John's gospel, however, we are able to read the testimony of another disciple who speaks of Peter's reinstatement.[251]

The episode occurs within the context of fishing. Peter and six other disciples went fishing one night. Early in the morning, they saw Jesus standing on the shore. Once he realized who it was, Peter jumped out of the boat and ran to Jesus.

In many ways, the early verses of John 21 show us the same old Peter. He takes charge and proclaims he is going fishing. The other disciples follow along. Once he realizes Jesus is on the shore, he hastily jumps out of the boat and rushes to see Him. He still loves his Lord and longs to be near Him.

The rest of the story, however, portrays Peter as a changed man. When Christ questioned Peter about his love and commitment, Peter was subdued in his responses. The old Peter would have boldly proclaimed his love, commitment, and loyalty to Jesus. The new Peter seems a bit sheepish as he professes his love. He does not claim to love Jesus more than the others. He does not even say he truly loves Jesus.

He responds to each of the three questions by simply affirming his love. The final time, he even called upon Christ as a witness, noting that Christ knew all things, therefore He knew of Peter's love.[252] Peter had learned that Christ knew him. He had also learned to temper his boldness with a submissive spirit.

Jesus' reaction to Peter is one filled with grace. John does not record Jesus scolding Peter, or even mentioning the denials. He did not need to say, "I told you so." He knew Peter's shame and guilt. He did not need to remind him of his own shortcoming.

Christ also responded to Peter with a challenge. Each time Peter replied to Christ's questions, Jesus told him to take care of His sheep.[253] Christ's words indicated that Peter's denial did not change the fact that Christ was going to build His church on Peter's testimony. Peter still had a significant role to fill in Christ's plans.

Christ also reminds Peter of the plan. Remember, Peter was quick to recognize Christ's glory, but did not want to see Christ's suffering. When Jesus reinstated Peter, He reaffirmed that there would be humility and suffering associated with His plan. He warned that Peter would lose his freedom. His final words recorded in that conversation with Peter are "follow me."[254]

Transformed and Utilized

Jesus' grace toward Peter is wonderfully reassuring to followers who have stumbled in their walk with Christ. Jesus demonstrates that He is ready to welcome into His fold all who are willing to submit to Him. Even though Peter had disowned Jesus, Jesus was ready to accept Him and utilize Him.

The Bible's record of Peter's life does not end on that shore. Peter was not only reinstated by Jesus, he was transformed by Jesus and used to proclaim Jesus' good news.

The change that occurred in Peter's life is truly amazing. On the night Jesus was arrested, Peter was overwhelmed with fear. He let that fear cause him to deny Jesus. After Pentecost, Peter no longer seemed to fear for his own well-being. He boldly proclaimed Jesus' gospel. He endured persecution and was even thrown in jail.[255]

Peter's letters indicated that he understood the need to submit to Christ and that the call to follow Him would include suffering. In 1 Peter, he wrote that followers of Christ should submit themselves to every authority.[256] Just a few sentences later he also wrote that Christ's followers are blessed, even if they suffer.[257] Those words are amazing when you consider that they were written by a man who at one time was unwilling to submit to Christ's plan because it included suffering.

Peter exercised effective leadership as he submitted Himself to Christ. He had been intimately associated with Christ, traveling with Him as a disciple for years. Through his denial, he learned that the boldness that comes with intimacy must be balanced by a willingness to submit to the Lord.

Christ can change a person. He took a man with all of Peter's flaws and transformed him into one of the primary leaders in the early church.

The story of Peter gives me hope. It teaches me that Christ can use people who misjudge their own integrity. It demonstrates that Jesus is willing to welcome back those who have stumbled in their walk with Him. It shows me that God can use the gifts and personalities He has given us to bear fruit in His Kingdom.

Questions for discussion/reflection:

What are some of the strengths and weaknesses you see in Peter? Do you see any of those characteristics in yourself?

What do you consider some essential attributes for a leader? How many leaders in the Bible fit your criteria?

How did Peter's denial of Christ change him? What are some mistakes that have changed you? How important is it that we confess our sins in order to learn from them?

What lessons about following would you like to learn from Peter's life?

Chapter 11
John: The Beloved Disciple

If you were assigned to be a career counselor for John, you would have a hard time putting together a resume. The stories of the gospel reveal a great deal about Peter's personality, but John is a more obscure figure. Even though he was one of Jesus' closest disciples, there is not much that distinguishes him from the rest.

You might try to describe who John was. You could note he was a fisherman prior to hearing Christ's call.[258] You could include family references; he was the brother of James and the son of Zebedee.[259] In the section that described his accomplishments, you might include some highlights from his time as a disciple. You could write that he sat closest to Jesus on the night of the Last Supper[260] and that he was the first of the twelve disciples to witness the empty tomb.[261] However, there are other stories that you would want to omit from the resume. You would avoid including the fact that his mother once spoke up for him to secure a place of honor in Christ's kingdom,[262] because you would not want others to think he needed his mom to advance his standing. You would not want to tell others that he and his brother once started an argument among the disciples.[263] You would even advise him to leave out the incident when he offered to obliterate an entire village of people.[264]

Peter's resume would be easy to develop. Water-walking and confessing Jesus as the Christ would be two quick highlights to pull out of a multitude of stories. John, on the other hand, is difficult to describe from the gospel stories. Peter is a prominent character in each of the gospel accounts. John is a prominent character in none of them. In fact, even in his own gospel account, John does not play a significant role. Unlike Peter, he is very willing to fade into the background and watch what happens in the life of Jesus.

If you had to introduce John to a prospective employer, you would do well to include the fact that he was an author. In his writings, we do not discover a great deal about His activity as a disciple, but we do gain insights about his understanding of Jesus' personality and ministry.

The Gospel according to John gives us a wonderful new perspective on Jesus' life. The first three gospels, Matthew, Mark, and Luke are very similar stories. John's account seems to come from a different perspective. If we did not have the gospel of John, we would not know the story of Jesus turning water into wine. We would probably think that Jesus' entire earthly ministry occurred within a year's time. We would not know the story of Peter's reconciliation with Jesus following the three denials on the night of Jesus' trial.

John completes the picture that we have of Jesus' ministry. It is in John's gospel that we find the boldest claims Jesus made about Himself. Furthermore, in the Gospel of John, we see a picture of a disciple who understands that Jesus was more than a mere man; He was God in the flesh. While Matthew, Mark, and Luke point us to Christ's divinity, it is in John that we find the most fully developed picture of Jesus' relationship with the Father and the Holy Spirit.

Despite his rather quiet personality, we can learn a great deal about following Christ from John. By comparing him to Peter, we see that not all followers of Christ will be bold and outspoken. Jesus can use people with a variety of gifts and personalities. He can use someone who is bold and outspoken like Peter, and he can use someone who is quiet and close, like John.

To Be Loved

In the Gospel of John, the author never identifies himself by name. He merely calls himself the disciple Jesus loved. In the Gospel of John, the beloved disciple played a unique role. He followed Jesus to places where other disciples did not go. He sat next to Jesus during the Last

Supper.[265] He was the only disciple standing by the cross when Jesus was crucified.[266] He was one of the first to witness the empty tomb.[267] He witnessed the reinstatement of Peter.[268]

Some may read the gospel of John and believe that John claims a high honor for himself by describing himself as the beloved disciple. We might read the Gospel of John with a bit of uneasiness, because we think that John has claimed that he was Jesus' favorite disciple. Maybe we think it is unfitting for a follower of Christ to claim such an honor for himself. After all, Jesus told us that we should not claim the seat of honor at a banquet, but to humble ourselves.[269] Was John being conceited when he called himself the beloved disciple?

By omitting his name, John was not claiming a special place of honor, but admitting the source of his hope. By leaving his name out of his own gospel account, John seems to direct attention away from himself. He identifies himself as one loved by the Lord. In John's Gospel, his personal identity is known in terms of his relationship with Jesus.

Most people desire to be identified by their names. John identified himself not by name, but by his relationship with Christ. I do not believe that he spoke out of conceit in calling himself the beloved disciple. He spoke of himself in submission to Christ. He set aside his own name to be identified with the Savior.

It is truly a great blessing to be loved by Jesus. One of the lessons we can learn from John is to treasure the love that Jesus has for us.

Many people have goals and dreams for their lives. They want houses or cars or advancement in their careers. They have plans that they are striving to complete. They want their lives to be filled with accomplishments and achievements. These people often want to be known by their accomplishments.

We often honor people for their accomplishments. When we hear the name of Dr. Martin Luther King Jr., we cannot help but think of his involvement in the civil rights movement. The name of Bill Gates immediately brings to mind the computer software produced by Microsoft. Ronald Reagan is known for his role as a United States President in the collapse of the Soviet Union. It is fitting that we remember these people for what they have accomplished.

John, however, does not claim any accomplishments of his own. He wants to be known for what Christ accomplished. He does not revel in his own glory, but he takes delight in Christ's glory shining on him. John treasured the fact that he was loved by Jesus. That is how he wanted others to think of him.

There is nothing wrong with having goals and dreams. God has used many goal-oriented people to accomplish incredible ministry in His Kingdom. But we must be careful that we do not become so wrapped up in our personal achievements that we lose sight of what Christ has achieved for us. Without the grace of Jesus, all of our temporary successes are meaningless.

A Different Kind of Disciple

I am glad that John and Peter are identified as two of the primary leaders in Christ's early church. The two of them offer a wonderful contrast to each other. Peter was bold and prone to stumble. John was quiet and willing to watch and learn. Peter boasted of his loyalty. John stayed by His Lord's side when all the other disciples abandoned Him.[270]

Peter's boldness was crucial to the beginning of the church. He preached to the crowds on Pentecost Sunday and thousands came to believe in the name of Jesus. John's silent, reflective nature became a blessing to followers of Christ through his writings, which are included in the Bible.

The story of the resurrection in John's Gospel[271] gives us a good picture of the contrast between Peter and John. On the morning of Christ's resurrection, Mary Magdalene came to Peter and John to tell them the tomb was empty. Peter and John both ran to the tomb. John arrived first, and stopped outside tomb. He looked inside to see what had happened. Throughout Jesus' ministry, John was a studious observer. He watched what Jesus did. From his gospel account, we see that he reflected on Jesus' life and work. He followed faithfully, even though we do not see him as an active or vocal leader.

Peter, on the other hand, rushed into the tomb. He was the second one to arrive, but he did not pause at the entrance. He walked inside and saw the linens and the burial cloth that had been around Jesus' head. Peter often acted impulsively. He was not a silent observer. He was an active and vocal participant. He often jumped to his own conclusions before he paused to think.

After Peter took the lead and ran into the tomb, John followed. John was not unwilling to be active, but he was not the natural leader that Peter was. John was blessed to have Peter as a fellow disciple. He benefited from Peter's willingness to be bold in approaching Christ.

Peter also benefited from John's gifts. While Peter was bold and quick to act, John's reflective nature helped him grow in understanding. Peter ran into the tomb first, but John's Gospel tells us that once John saw the inside of the tomb, he understood and believed.[272]

John's intimacy with Christ was a benefit to Peter at the Last Supper. In his boldness, Peter wanted to know the identity of the betrayer. However, he did not venture to ask Jesus himself. Instead, he asked John to make the inquiry.[273]

While Peter was bold, John was content to be known as the one Jesus loved. He seemed to take pleasure in sitting at Jesus' feet. The gifts and abilities of Peter and John complemented each other very well. Peter was quick to act. John was thoughtful and reflective. Both of these men loved their Lord and Savior. Both desired to be faithful to Christ. Both were used by Christ to build His church.

Followers of Christ are called to imitate Him. But this does not mean that all of Christ's followers will be an army of interchangeable parts. We are not exact replicas of each other. God has created us with different gifts. He can use the gifts of people who have temperaments as different as Peter and John.

The Beauty of Silence

John was a rather silent disciple. The Gospels only record John speaking on a few occasions.[274] On many of the occasions when he is quoted, he is speaking with other disciples, or on behalf of other disciples. In the book of Acts, his silence seems to continue. Early in that book, he frequently traveled with Peter, but Peter did most of the talking.

John's silence was not an indication of apathy. He studiously observed Christ's ministry. He was a witness to many events that other disciples did not see.[275] In many ways, he sat silently at Jesus feet and was shaped as he observed Jesus.

Many people today feel guilty because they believe they should be doing more. There are numerous opportunities to volunteer and be useful. Many wonderful organizations would love to have people commit their time. Schools, hospitals, churches, political campaigns, and nursing homes are just some of the places that will ask you to donate your time. You might like to spend more time with neighbors, invite more people to your home, be more active with family members, but you feel like you just do not have enough time. You might feel like you are letting people down, because you would like to do more. Maybe you believe you are lazy or a poor manager of your time.

John is a wonderfully uplifting character for people who feel like they can never do enough. John is not remembered for incredible acts of mercy or for bold preaching. He was a silent observer. He meditated on Christ's ministry.

After the birth of Jesus, His mother, Mary, treasured the memories and pondered them in her heart.[276] She did not immediately tell the whole world what had happened. That was not her role in Christ's ministry. She had been used by God to bring His son into the world; others were given the job of proclaiming His Kingdom.

Similarly, when Christ was dining at the home of Mary and Martha, Mary was praised for simply sitting at Jesus' feet and listening.[277] Martha was busy preparing dinner and tending to all of the details that seem so significant when one has company. Mary did not help. She did not offer Jesus a drink. She did not get the chairs for the disciples. There were so many things that she could have done, but she merely sat at Jesus' feet and listened. Jesus said that in her silence, she had chosen a better way.

The writer of Psalm 46 was instructed to "be still, and know that I am God."[278] Our busyness can be a distraction in our lives. We can fill our time with so many good things that we miss out on the best things. Even our activities for church or other worthy causes can become a hindrance to our walk with God.

I have gone through periods in my life when I have been very busy. I have led youth groups, studied at Christian institutions, and volunteered to teach Sunday School class; all the while neglecting my devotional life. I may have prayed at mealtimes and read my Bible at the beginning of the Sunday School class, but I took no time to be still in God's presence. My walk with God has suffered because of such busyness.

Even Jesus took time to be alone with God. In the midst of His ministry, He would send the crowds away so that He could be alone with His Father.[279] Jesus' ministry was filled with parables, debates, teaching and healing; but He also made it a priority to be still in the presence of His Father.

John imitates Christ's stillness. John is silent as He stands by Jesus and observes. It is no coincidence that John was the one who looked at the empty tomb and believed. John's silent persistence in following Christ allowed him to be at the cross to hear Jesus' instruction to take care of His mother.[280]

Are you too busy to hear the instruction of God? Is your life so full of activity that you do not have time to be still in God's presence? If so, your activity might make you feel good, but you are missing what is best. Even though John was a relatively silent disciple, when Christ called him to action, he was prepared to follow.

Paying Attention to God

"Most men are more eager to listen to the world than to God."[281] The world's priorities are clearly known. Television shows teach us to value beauty and wealth. We are convinced that hard work is worthwhile because it will advance our status in the eyes of others. News reports tell us about the political and economic environment around us. The voice of the world is hard to ignore. It screams so that we cannot help but pay attention.

God speaks more subtly. He does not scream to force us to listen. He whispers so that we have to respond with an effort to listen. We have to be still in God's presence so the screams of the world do not drown out His message.

Many Christians practice the art of meditation. Meditation is not some mysterious cultic practice that allows us to become superhumans. It is merely spending time in silence to think about matters of God. It is allowing time to focus our daydreams on God's will for our lives. When we make a habit to spend time in silence—whether that silence is meditation or prayer or devotional reading or Bible study—we are allowing time for God to be a priority. We are allowing His will to shape us. We are setting aside the screams of the world to be captivated by His leading.

Paying attention to God does not happen accidentally. We must make an effort to listen to Him. But the effort is worthwhile. The effort to listen will make us set aside the clutter in our lives. The effort to listen will prepare us to hear God's voice and respond faithfully.

Followers of Christ can learn from John, who was willing to sit by Jesus' side, content to follow Him, and ready to serve once Christ gave clear instruction.

The Bible's last record of John places him in exile on the Island of Patmos.[282] He was put into exile because of his testimony. In the Gospels he was a silent leader. But God had a plan for him. That plan included writing a fourth Gospel, which completed the picture of Christ's ministry. It included three letters to the church that encouraged Christ's followers to follow Him faithfully. It resulted in his exile. Christ's ministry shaped John so that He became a significant character in the development of God's early church.

God uses people like John, who are willing to listen attentively and wait patiently for His clear instruction.

Questions for discussion/reflection:

What are the similarities between Peter and John? What are the differences?

FOLLOW THE LEADER

Why do you think John refers to himself as the beloved disciple?

What can John's example teach you about filling you life with busy activities?

Why is meditation such a difficult practice? How would you benefit from periods of time that you devote to silent reflection?

Chapter 12
Thomas: Faithful Pessimist

You probably know him as "Doubting Thomas."

I think Thomas gets an unfair shake from most contemporary Christians, because he is only remembered for his skepticism. He receives the title of being a doubter because of one solitary incident after Christ's resurrection. When the other disciples told Thomas that Jesus had appeared, he did not believe them. Because he was unable to imagine his master living after He had been crucified, he went so far as to say that he would never believe Jesus had risen unless he was able to put his hands in the scars on Jesus' body.[283] For this comment, he will forever be known as "Doubting Thomas."

I believe the nickname is unfair, because Thomas' response to Jesus is actually much more forceful than the response of the other disciples. In the Gospel of Mark, we learn that Jesus rebuked all of the disciples for not believing the testimony of others who had seen him.[284] In Luke, we read that when Jesus appeared to the disciples, they all had to see him eat before they believed.[285] In contrast, Thomas believed as soon as he saw Jesus. Upon seeing Him, Thomas reacted by confessing that Jesus was his Lord and his God.[286]

Thomas' doubts were understandable. There was no incident ever recorded of a man sentenced to death coming back from the grave. The fact that he was skeptical about Christ's resurrection serves as evidence to the reality that Jesus did come back from the grave. His doubts are echoed by many today. Many do not believe it was possible for Jesus to rise from the dead. They try to explain the resurrection as a hoax or an outright lie. When we see Thomas' reaction to the resurrected Lord, the possibility of a scandal seems minimal.

Thomas was a realist. Peter struggled because he could not accept Jesus' suffering. Thomas' struggle was just the opposite. He understood the humanity and suffering of Jesus, but he had difficulty seeing His glory.[287] Yet Christ was able to transform this skeptic into a powerful witness for His Kingdom.

Faithful Realist

We don't have too much information about Thomas. The Gospels of Matthew, Mark, and Luke merely list Thomas as one of the disciples.[288] John's Gospel gives us more information about Thomas. He is mentioned in three stories, and in all of these stories, we see a disciple who has a pessimistic outlook.

The first time John mentions Thomas is just after Jesus and His disciples learn of the death of their friend, Lazarus. Jesus started moving toward Jerusalem after they hear of the death, and Thomas commented that they should follow so that they could die with Him.[289] Thomas knew that the Jewish leaders were not fond of Jesus. He realized that Jesus could be putting His life in danger by moving toward Jerusalem. Rather than running in fear, he demonstrated resolve to follow his Master, even though he might face death.

The second time we read of Thomas in John's Gospel is when Jesus is teaching His disciples about the future Kingdom. After Jesus told His followers that they knew the way to the place He was going, Thomas spoke up. He spoke for all of the disciples as he admitted, "Lord, we don't know where you are going, so how can we know the way?"[290]

I must admit that I admire Thomas for this question. I can remember being in school, and hearing my teacher use words I did not understand. Rather than raising my hand and asking for clarification, I pretended to know what the teacher was talking about. When I did this, I quickly became lost in the discussion. I did not know what I was supposed to be learning.

Whenever I was lost in a class discussion, I always appreciated a fellow student who would ask for clarification. That student may have risked looking foolish, but she helped everyone in class by asking her question.

Thomas asked a question that helps all followers of Christ. How do we know the way? Jesus answered that we know the way when we know Him, because He is the way.[291] If we want to know how to get to the Father, we follow Him.

In this incident, Thomas set the tone for other disciples to ask questions. Philip followed Thomas by asking Jesus to simply show them the Father.[292] Through this conversation, followers of Christ are blessed today by a chapter of scripture that helps us understand Jesus more fully. In this passage, we learn that Jesus is the way to the Father, and that there is a mysterious union between Jesus and the Father. The church has been blessed by this chapter of scripture, a chapter that started with Thomas asking a question.

Thomas was willing to risk embarrassment in order to gain understanding. He was willing to struggle with Jesus' words in order to grow closer to Him. In similar situations, many people may be content to nod their heads and pretend to understand. Not Thomas. He asked questions that are still helping us today.

The third time we meet Thomas in the Gospel of John is when he heard from the other disciples that they had seen the risen Lord.[293] Thomas had not been with the other disciples when Jesus first appeared to them. The rest of them had the privilege of seeing with their own eyes that Jesus had risen. When Thomas was reunited with the other disciples, they told him what they had seen. In no uncertain terms, he let the other disciples know that he did not believe their story. He needed irrefutable proof before he would believe that Jesus was alive.

The Bible tells us that one week later; Jesus appeared to the disciples again. This time Thomas was with them. I wish I could have been there during that week between Christ's two visits. How did Thomas interact with the other disciples? Were there arguments or discussions about Christ's resurrection? Were the other disciples disgusted by Thomas' skepticism?

I am impressed that Thomas was with the disciples one week later. A disagreement over the resurrection of Christ is enough to cause many close friendships to disintegrate. But Thomas was with the other disciples, despite his unbelief.

Thomas had his doubts, but he was loyal. When he thought Jesus might die, he called others to follow Christ with Him, even if it meant his own death.[294] When he did not understand Jesus' teaching, he asked difficult questions so that He would know the way to get where Jesus was going.[295] When he doubted the disciples' testimony, he did not abandon them, but continued to meet with them.[296]

In some ways, Thomas is a wonderful example for Christians today. We will have struggles and doubts. We will not always understand what God is doing. When we face those times of trial and misunderstanding, do we run from Christ, or do we remain loyal? God can use people who are skeptical, if they remain faithful to Him. Thomas remained faithful despite his doubts. He submitted himself to Christ even though he did not understand. He followed Christ even when it looked like following would lead to death.

Happy Christians

Too many people believe that following Christ is the instant solution to every problem. People often turn to Christ in the midst of a crisis, and believe that the benefit to following Christ must be immediately recognized. A baseball player might testify that his batting average went up after he became a Christian. A business woman might excitedly tell you how she received two promotions shortly after she started attending church. A research scientist may profess that he was able to create a wonderful sugar free sweetener after spending hours in prayer. There are many people who are filled with excitement about their faith in Christ because they believe they have seen God act in their lives. They are filled with joy and enthusiasm because they have experienced success in their pursuits.

However, faithful followers do not always experience immediate gratification. Some prayers are never answered the way we want them to be.[297] Job was a man who was faithful to God, but he endured terrible struggle in his life.[298]

I fear many Christians cheapen the good news of the Gospel when they turn following Christ into quick fix for our earthly struggles. God can, and often does, perform incredible miracles. I know people who have been healed from illnesses in a way that doctors cannot explain. I have seen God work to miraculously transform hearts. However, not every incident in our lives will be a wonderfully positive experience. We will endure suffering and death. We will struggle with our sinful nature. We will have to pick up our crosses to follow Christ.[299] The promise of the Gospel is not that we will never have to suffer. In fact, following Christ will often bring suffering. The good news is that when we are united with Christ, we can be assured that nothing will separate us from the love of God.[300]

Thomas was a faithful follower despite his pessimism. He did not follow Christ with the false illusion that every second of his life will be filled with blissful pleasure. He understood the reality of suffering. He understood that Christ could suffer and die. Yet he followed faithfully.

There are many wonderful passages of scripture that tell us of the joy of God's strength. Sometimes, we misread these passages. Scripture tells us, "the joy of the Lord is my strength."[301] "I can do everything through Him who strengthens me."[302] "Those who hope in the Lord...will soar on wings like eagles."[303] These verses can be wonderfully reassuring, but they do not promise that there will never be tears in our lives.

I have known people who have read these verses and concluded that if they truly believe in Jesus then they will never be sad. They will always be filled with joy. They believe that any sorrow they experience is a direct result of their lack of faith.

I feel sad for people who believe that the Christian faith prohibits them from feeling sorrow. They take the passages of joy and strength and misinterpret them. They wrongly believe that God will protect them from any sadness, when scripture is teaching them that God will give them strength to endure any sadness.

One of my favorite passages of scripture is Isaiah 40:28-31. This is one of the passages that I believe is often misread. One of the ways I see it being misread is in the way so many people omit the final two lines. We often read, "Those who hope in the Lord will renew their strength. They will soar on wings like eagles." I have seen this text inscribed into beautiful wooden carvings. I have considered purchasing a picture of an eagle soaring over beautiful scenery with those words written underneath. However, I have not yet purchased that picture. I want the rest of that text inscribed in that wood or written under that picture. The rest of the text says, "They will run and not grow weary, they will walk and not be faint."

Most of us like the idea of God's power causing us to soar on wings like eagles. We like the elation of being in God's presence. We are pleased by the thought that God's power will lift us above the fretting and struggling of this world and land us safely on the other side. Thankfully, God does lift us to incredible heights in our walk with Him. We can experience wonderful communion with Him as we follow Christ. But hope in the Lord does not lead exclusively to soaring experiences.

Sometimes hoping in the Lord allows us the strength to run without growing weary. We are still called to put forth effort as we endure the struggles of life, but God gives us strength to sustain us. We may not always experience the soaring sensation, but He is still granting His strength.

Other times, our struggles can seem so overwhelming that it requires all of our effort to walk through them without falling or fainting. When we endure struggles in this manner, it is good to remember that the strength to endure came from God. God promises strength, but that strength does not always lead to soaring success. Sometimes it seems like just barely enough.

Struggling With God

Struggles are common, even for people who are faithful to God. In fact, struggles are so common, that God made sure that we have examples of how we can pray when we are struggling. The book of

Psalms is filled with complaints of struggling. "How long, O Lord, will you forget me forever?"[304] "My God, my God, why have you forsaken me? Why are you so far from saving me, so far from the words of my groaning?"[305] "You have taken my companions and loved ones from me; the darkness is my closest friend."[306]

The Psalmist was familiar with suffering, and many Psalms were written by David, who was described as fully devoted to God.[307] In the midst of his struggling, the Psalmist cries out to God. Sometimes, those cries seem irreverent. Those complaints seem to be skeptical. But God does not rebuke the Psalmist for his audacity. The Psalms are models for our prayers. We can turn to God in difficult times with the words of the Psalms. We do not have to pretend to be filled with joy when we are really filled with sorrow. God wants to hear our prayers. He wants our hearts to be devoted to Him. The presence of sadness does not mean we are rebelling against God. Christ calls us to come to Him with our heavy hearts to find rest.[308]

Thomas did not pretend to be upbeat and optimistic in the midst of his fears and doubts. He did not need to fear, but neither did he have to pretend to be happy when his heart was heavy.

Christ's call in our lives will not mean that we will constantly experience the bliss of eternal joy. When we are saddened, followers of Christ may feel free to approach the throne of God with their concerns.

People do not like to hear complaints or concerns. If I have a complaint about a television program, I may write a letter, but I am doubtful that it will be taken seriously. I have the impression that the people who would read my letter would politely dismiss my concerns. They might write me a response that told me they valued my opinions. They would probably tell me that they feel badly that I have a complaint. But they probably would not do much to address my concerns.

God is not in the business of dismissing our concerns. He listens to our prayers. He cares about His children. He might not give us everything we want, but He responds to our needs with His grace. Job was very open about his complaints and struggles. He voiced his concerns to God in prayer, and God said that Job had spoken appropriately.[309]

Followers of Christ do not need to feel defensive when fellow followers are bold in voicing their concerns. Christians will not always be optimistic about the immediate future. We will face trial and temptation. God does not try to hush us when we voice our concerns. He is not offended by our cries for His help.

Thomas was not known for his optimism. He voiced his concerns and doubts. But he was loyal to Christ despite those concerns.

The Gospel's Power to Overcome Doubts

Whenever we hear about Thomas' doubts, our immediate reaction is to say something like, "It is too bad that Thomas was such a doubter. Why couldn't he simply believe? He should have known that Jesus was going to come back to life."

Whenever we focus on Thomas' doubts, we are missing the primary point of the story of Christ appearing to him.[310] This story is not told to teach us that Thomas had doubt, but to teach us that the power of Christ's resurrection is able to overcome the deepest doubts.

Thomas was reasonable in his doubts. The resurrection of a person who had been crucified had never been reported prior to Christ. It is not common for people to come back to life. The thought of Christ living again was unthinkable. Doubt was a reasonable reaction.

The story of Christ appearing to Thomas teaches us that Christ has the power to shatter reasonable doubts. Thomas had been bold in his persistence to disbelieve. He claimed that he would need to touch Jesus' scars and see his wounds before his doubt would subside. One week later, his doubt was immediately shattered. The Bible does not report Thomas placing his hands on Jesus' scars, but immediately professing that Jesus was his Lord and God. His profession went beyond merely believing that Jesus was alive. He claimed that Jesus was God Himself.

Immediately following the story of Thomas' doubts, the Gospel of John goes on to explain that, "Jesus did many other miraculous signs in the presence of His disciples, which are not recorded in this book. But these are written that you may believe that Jesus is the Christ, the Son of God, and that by believing you may have life in His name."[311]

The story of Thomas' doubt is told so that we might be convinced that Jesus is our only hope for everlasting life. Thomas' doubt is an interesting story, but if we become overly concerned about his doubts, we may miss the resounding claim that Jesus conquered death. Thomas' doubt can represent our own doubts. Just as Christ's presence shattered Thomas' doubts, His power can overcome our concerns, so that even though we have not seen, we can be blessed as we believe.[312]

Exalted Status

After Thomas' confession of Christ, His status changed. Prior to his confession, he was one of many disciples. In fact, if the story of Thomas' doubts had not been included in the Gospel of John, we probably would not pay much attention to him.

In the story following Thomas' confession, a group of disciples went fishing. Thomas was one of the fishermen that night. When John listed the disciples who went fishing, he listed Thomas second. Prior to Thomas' confession, he was never listed very highly on the list of disciples. Peter was usually listed first. James and John were usually listed second and third. Thomas normally appeared somewhere down the list. After his doubts and subsequent confession, he was listed second. His confession raised his status. His temporary doubts did not damage his value or membership with the other disciples. The fact that Christ changed his heart made his name known.

Like Thomas, all followers of Christ have their status exalted when they confess Jesus is their Lord and their God. Our doubts and fears of the past do not stand in the way of our walk with Him. We may approach Christ with our fears, and we can be assured that His grace will be sufficient to change us.

The story of Thomas shows us that Christ can use people who might be prone to doubts and concerns. His power can shatter our doubts. Confessing His name exalts our standing in God's Kingdom.

Questions for discussion/reflection:
Do you think it is fair that the Apostle Thomas is known as Doubting Thomas? Why or why not?

How does "being realistic" affect your faith? Does realism ever strengthen you faith? When does it hinder your walk with Christ?

Thomas was not afraid to ask questions. Do you ever try to hide your ignorance by pretending to understand? How does this affect your growth?

Does following Christ always lead to instant gratification? How should we respond to God when we struggle with uncertainty?

Chapter 13
Judas Iscariot: Rebellion

I am a fan of the Chicago Cubs, and I have been for most of my life. When they succeed, I feel an unjustifiable sense of pride. When they perform poorly, I feel an unexplainable frustration that permeates my day. My childhood was filled with summer afternoons spent watching the Cubs on television. I can still recite the starting lineup from the 1984 team. Even today, if the Cubs are on television, I make an effort to watch the game.

Some of my friends poke fun at my devotion to the Cubs. They tease me when the Cubs lose, and mockingly congratulate me when the Cubs win. They know I am a fan. However, I must confess that I do not believe I am devoted to the Cubs. I consider myself a fair-weather fan at best. I only pay close attention when they are doing well. If they begin to falter, I quickly become frustrated and lose interest.

Most fans are not particularly devoted. Fans will flock to stadiums when their team is doing well. But losing teams play in front of empty seats.

Jesus was not looking for fans when He came to earth; He was looking for devoted followers. There is a huge difference between a fan and a fully devoted follower. Fans will marvel at success. They watch with awe as amazing feats are being accomplished. However, fans quickly lose interest once difficulties begin. Fully devoted followers are loyal when circumstances seem hopeless. Their cheering does not change to heckling when they do not like what is happening.

It is easy to be a fan of a Savior who heals, comforts, and performs amazing signs and wonders. But applauding the successes of our Savior does not make a person a fully devoted follower. People who merely cheer successes are nothing more than fair-weather fans.

Despite His call for people to follow Him, Jesus had a number of people surrounding Him who were merely fans. The Gospel of John teaches us that many people started to follow Jesus because they were amazed by His miraculous signs and wonders. He turned water into wine.[313] He healed the son of a government official.[314] He healed a man who had been disabled for thirty-eight years.[315] Each of these miracles caused more people to pay attention to Christ's ministry. At one point, over five thousand people were following Him, and they were delighted when He performed another miracle to feed them.[316]

Many of these people were not fully devoted followers. They were fans because they liked to see what Jesus was doing. They were impressed by His power and got caught up in the frenzy that developed around Jesus. The reports of His successful ministry of miracles caused people to follow Him when He wanted to be alone. There were even rumblings about giving Jesus political power.[317]

Christ realized that the devotion of the crowds was shallow. They were not devoted to Him, they were merely His fans. In chapter 6 of John's Gospel, Jesus confronted the lack of devotion. He revealed the motives of His followers. He explained that they were following Him because He fed them and performed miracles.[318]

Jesus wanted more for His followers. He wanted them to pursue Him. He wanted them to be committed to Him. In a bold move, Jesus explained to the crowds that they should long for something greater than signs and wonders. He revealed that He had come from heaven to bring them food that would eternally satisfy. His flesh and blood would be food that nourished them.[319]

The crowds had a hard time accepting Jesus' words.[320] His teaching was difficult to understand. How could anyone give His flesh and blood for others to eat? The crowds had been thrilled by His miracles, but were bothered by His teaching. They liked the signs and wonders, but they were put off by His hard words. They were merely fans, and showed their true nature by walking away once they no longer viewed Jesus as a success story.[321]

Today, there are many people who are mere fans of Jesus. They turn to Him for miraculous intervention when they are sick or hurting. They pray for money and power and earthly success. They might even be pleased when their hopes are realized. They see Jesus as someone who can help them. They will follow Him as a fan when they are pleased by His performance, but they will stop following once Jesus calls for a response. They do not want to hear Jesus call them to pick up a cross or anything else that might be slightly uncomfortable.

Judas Iscariot Revealed

Out of the five thousand who had followed Jesus, only twelve were identified after He called them to greater devotion. Yet not all of the twelve were fully committed to following Jesus. One of them was a devil[322] who continued to remain near Jesus despite his lack of commitment. Even though Judas remained near Jesus, his devotion never seemed to develop beyond the level of a fan. He had been impressed by Jesus' miracles, but He proved himself to be a traitor.

The account of Judas Iscariot is one of the most perplexing stories in the Bible. He was so close, and yet so far away. He had the advantage of knowing Jesus personally and being one of Jesus' twelve closest followers. He witnessed Christ's miracles, traveled with Jesus, served as the treasurer for the group,[323] and allowed Jesus to wash his feet.[324] Yet in spite of this opportunity to grow near to Christ, Judas faltered. He did not submit to Jesus, and he committed one of the most infamous acts of betrayal in the history of the world.

The life of Judas should be a warning for us. We can never know what went through his mind, but we can be warned that you can mingle with other followers without being committed to Christ. You can be impressed by Jesus' power without submitting to Him as Lord. You can be a fan of Jesus without being a fully devoted follower.

Even though Judas followed Jesus, He was not fully devoted to Him. Judas had his own agenda. He was more interested in obtaining wealth than in honoring His Lord.[325] Judas knew Jesus well enough to predict His movements,[326] but did not recognize Him as God.

As we consider the relationship between Jesus and Judas Iscariot, we should be warned that as long as we cling to our desires, we cannot be fully devoted to Jesus. We must take care that our own ideas and agendas do not cause us to stumble as we follow Him.

Interested Onlooker

I wish I had a window into the mind of Judas Iscariot. I would like to know why he followed Christ for years, only to betray Him. Did he plan betrayal from the beginning? Did he believe he was truly committed to Christ? Did he follow merely out of curiosity? Was he a tool of the devil from the very beginning? Did he know what kind of treachery he was committing?

There is little doubt that Judas had an interest in Jesus' ministry. He shared a lot in common with Jesus' other followers. He was Jewish, and may have longed for the messiah that God had promised in the Old Testament. He may have had expectations for that Messiah to free the Jewish people from Roman authority.

Judas Iscariot continued to follow Jesus when many others left, but in John's Gospel, he was identified as a traitor the first time he was mentioned. He was interested enough in Jesus' ministry to continue traveling with Him, but he was not committed enough to submit to Christ. When Jesus began to be pursued by the religious leaders, Judas found a way to turn His position among Christ's disciples into a profit. He may have been impressed by Christ, but he was not impressed enough to be loyal when others wanted to see Him dead.

When Christ calls us to follow Him, He is calling us to more than an association with His group. Christ is not pacified by people who try to fit in a church and adopt some worthwhile causes. Judas looked like the other disciples. He voiced concern for the poor.[327] He may have been a fan of Christ, but he was not faithful.

Christ wants His followers to be wholeheartedly devoted to Him. Even when we do not understand what Christ is doing in our lives, we are called to submit to Him.

Two Predictions

I am struck by the similarities between Judas Iscariot and Peter. Both of these men were followers of Jesus. Both of them were Jewish. Both of them objected to events or teachings in Christ's ministry.[328] Both of them turned away from Christ on the night of His trial. In spite of the similarities, the direction of their lives could not have been more different following Christ's crucifixion. Jesus urged Peter to take care of His church,[329] yet he said that it would have been better for Judas if he had never been born.[330]

The similarities and differences between Judas and Peter are highlighted on the night of Jesus' betrayal. In the events that surrounded the Last Supper, Jesus made two predictions about His disciples. Both predictions are recorded in each of the Gospels. The first prediction was made for all to hear; one of Jesus' disciples would betray their master.[331] The disciples' curiosity was aroused by this revelation. They immediately wanted to know the identity of the betrayer. Jesus subtly pointed out that Judas was the betrayer. He made it evident to Judas that he knew his intentions. The second prediction was made directly to Peter. After Peter declared his loyalty to his Master, Jesus revealed that Peter would deny knowing Jesus three times before the rooster crowed.[332]

Two Acts of Betrayal

Before that night was over, both of Jesus' predictions were fulfilled. Judas betrayed Jesus with an infamous kiss. Peter denied knowing Jesus three times. Matthew 26-27 tells the stories of these two acts of treason.

Judas' betrayal was planned and executed. He had met with leaders prior to Jesus' prediction.[333] His heart had been hardened against his teacher. He knew that his actions were an act of betrayal. He accepted thirty pieces of silver to intentionally rebel against the Lord.

Peter's act was not planned, but was born in a moment of fear. He had expressed an intention to be loyal to his Master, and there is no reason to doubt his sincerity. However, when the moment came that he was asked whether or not he was with Jesus, he denied knowing Jesus. Each time he disowned Jesus, his denials grew in their intensity. Eventually, he even cursed and swore that he did not know the man.[334]

The actions of these two men cause us to reflect on the nature of sin. Sin can be planned or it can be spontaneous. Often, like Judas, we know the difference between right and wrong. Despite our understanding, we rebel. We intentionally turn our back on Christ and choose what is wrong. We might try to justify our actions. We may believe that our plans are better than God's plan. We might rationalize that sin is permissible, because we can ask for forgiveness after the fact.

Jesus calls us to deny ourselves in order to follow Him.[335] He knew that we would face instances when we have to choose between submitting to Him and submitting to our own desires. Judas, knowing the treachery of his actions, chose to submit to his own desires and betray Jesus. If we are not ready to deny our own desires, we can fall prey to the same trap.

We can be guilty of intentional rebellion, like Judas. We can also be guilty of giving in to our momentary weakness, like Peter. The emotions of a given moment can overwhelm us, and cause us to lose sight of the difference between right and wrong. Peter was likely afraid for his life, and this fear caused him to lie. Other emotions can make us lose sight of the good we want to do. Lust, fear, and anger can easily cause moments of clouded judgment when we fall away from Christ in ways that we would not have thought possible. We may fully intend to follow Christ, yet we still stumble and fall. Realizing our weakness can be a humbling experience.

In order to avoid sins caused by momentary lapses in judgment, God has always taught His people to keep His Word before their eyes. In the Old Testament, the people of Israel were taught to discuss the commandments constantly, to wear reminders of God's laws on their hands and to place symbols on their doorframes.[336] These constant reminders were preemptive strikes against momentary lapses. If we are not immersed in God's word, we can be ruled by our impulsive emotions, rather than our commitment to following Christ.

Repentance and Remorse

Judas and Peter were both guilty of sinning against their Lord. Each of them realized that they were guilty of sin. Each of them felt badly about their actions. One of them responded by taking his own life,[337] the other was eventually reinstated as Christ's disciple.[338]

Remorse and repentance are two different things. When a person feels remorseful, she feels badly about something she did. When a person is repentant, her remorse leads her to seek reconciliation with the person she has harmed.

Peter felt remorseful for his act of denying Christ. He went out and wept bitterly.[339] Humbled by the recognition of his weakness, he returned to Christ's group of followers. He waited in the place where He met Christ. After Christ's resurrection, he had an opportunity to be reconciled to Christ. His remorse led him to repentance and reconciliation. He realized that he could not undo his sin. He could not fix the damage it had done to his relationship with Jesus. His only hope was Christ's gracious willingness to receive him back. Peter was not disappointed. Christ's capacity to forgive and receive is unlimited. When we turn away from our sin and turn to Him, Christ forgives and reconciles us to Himself.

Like Peter, once Judas saw that Jesus had been condemned to die, he felt remorseful.[340] But instead of turning to Christ, he tried to make things right on his own. He went to the chief priests and returned the silver. He asked them to release Jesus, but they refused. Some sins cannot be easily undone. Judas gave his best effort to undo the consequences of his rebellion. I believe he truly did feel badly about his actions, but it was beyond his ability to make it right. Christ had been betrayed and sentenced. Judas could no longer help him. We might give Judas some credit for making the effort to correct his actions, but he did not repent of his sin. He did not repent and turn to Christ. His feeling of guilt was genuine; in fact his remorse was so great that it caused him to hang himself. However, his feelings of remorse and own efforts to redeem himself were insufficient to undo the damage.

Judas failed to turn to Christ with his own guilt. He realized that he could not undo his betrayal, and he gave up on his Teacher. By taking his own life, he ended the possibility of seeking restoration. The result of his remorse was not repentance. He did not humble Himself in Christ's presence and ask for forgiveness.

Christ is willing to forgive those who sin against Him. He even asked God to forgive the people who crucified Him.[341] However, people who intentionally sin against Christ are often unwilling to repent and receive Christ's forgiveness.

In his book, What's So Amazing About Grace? Philip Yancey tells the story of a friend who planned to leave his wife and children for a new woman. Before he committed this terrible act, he considered the effect it would have on his walk with God. He knew that he was plotting to do something evil, and he wondered if God would be able to forgive him later. Yancey responded to his friend with these words.

> "Can God forgive you? Of course. You know the Bible. God uses murderers and adulterers. For goodness' sake, a couple of scoundrels named Peter and Paul led the New Testament church. Forgiveness is *our* problem, not God's. What we have to go through to commit sin distances us from God—we change in the very act of rebellion—and there is no guarantee we will ever come back. You ask me about forgiveness now, but will you even want it later, especially if it involves repentance?"[342]

God can forgive our sins, even our sins of rebellion. The question is, will we want to be forgiven? Will we repent? Intentionally rebelling against Christ is not a danger because it makes God unwilling to forgive, but it may change us into people who are unwilling to repent and accept His forgiveness.

Judas started out as a fan of Christ. He was drawn, like many others, by the signs and wonders that Jesus performed. However, when Judas was faced with the decision to submit to Christ or submit to his personal desires, he chose to rebel. He intentionally turned away from Jesus, and never turned back to Him again.

Following Christ calls us to set aside our own desires. When we fail, Christ is willing to forgive. However, if we are mere fans, rather than fully devoted followers, it will be difficult for us to repent, despite our remorseful feelings. Following Christ means we acknowledge He is Lord, and that His plans and abilities exceed our own thoughts and desires.

Questions for discussion/reflection:

What are some hard words that Jesus spoke that still cause us to question Him?

How can you be sure that you are truly devoted to Jesus, and not merely a fan?

What is the difference between Peter's denial of Christ and Judas' betrayal?

If God is willing to forgive any sin, why is it such a problem if we intentionally decide to turn away from Him?

Chapter 14
Paul: A Turnaround Story

In the book of Acts, the number of Jesus' followers grows exponentially. In the opening chapter, approximately 120 people are identified as followers of Christ.[343] By the end of the book, the good news of Jesus had been proclaimed in many major cities from Jerusalem to Rome. Followers of Christ had started churches in many different cities around the world.

As the number of Christ's followers grew, new leaders began to emerge within His church. It is likely that many of the new leaders mentioned in Acts never met Christ prior to His resurrection. People such as Timothy, Barnabas, John Mark, Silas, and Titus are identified as leaders in the early church even though they are never mentioned in the Gospels.[344]

One leader in the early church, Paul, gets special attention for his role in the advancement of the Gospel. The stories of Paul's ministry occupy a major portion of the book of Acts, and Paul's letters to Christians around the world comprise a great deal of our New Testament. In fact, Paul is recognized as the human author of more books in the Bible than anyone else.[345] It is difficult to imagine what the New Testament would look like if Paul had never become a follower of Christ.

A Sordid Past

Ironically, Paul was not always a devoted follower of Christ. The first time he is mentioned in the Bible, he is identified with a group of people who were persecuting followers of Christ.[346] He was present when Stephen, a deacon in the early church, was murdered for his faith.[347] He had worked to throw men and women into prison for their faith in Christ.[348] He considered himself an enemy of the followers of Christ, because he believed they were corrupting the Jewish teachings about the One True God.

Paul was a zealous individual. He believed he was persecuting the church because of his devotion to God. He had been trained under a well-known Pharisee, Gamaliel.[349] He considered himself a Pharisee and a devout Jew. He had been raised according to all of the Jewish laws, and desired that these laws be observed steadfastly.[350] His resume as a devout Jew was impeccable. He considered himself a righteous man even by the most legalistic of standards. Furthermore, Paul was a Roman citizen.[351] This privilege allowed him to travel around the country with the assurance that if he were arrested, he would get a fair hearing.

Paul seemed to be the prototypical enemy of Christ's followers. As a Jew, he wanted to see the Old Testament teachings proclaimed, and the good news of Jesus seemed to be a corruption of his beliefs. As a Roman citizen, he would want the uprising of unauthorized religions to be subdued.

Paul worked feverishly to persecute the church. After he became a follower of Christ, he would look back at his life with sadness. He would call himself the least of the Apostles, because he had persecuted the church.[352] Even though Paul was confident that Christ had forgiven him and called him to be a leader in the church, he was humbled by his early association with the persecutors of Christ's church.

True Conversion

The story of Paul's conversion is found in Acts 9. After securing permission from the high priest, Paul began a journey to Damascus to arrest Christ's followers. Along the way, he was blinded by a light and heard the voice of Jesus. Jesus told Paul to stop the persecution. He told Paul to go into the city and wait for further instructions. Paul went to Damascus, blinded by this encounter.

In Damascus, God spoke to a man named Ananias, a follower of Christ. God told him to seek out Paul, the persecutor of Christians, and lay hands on him to restore his sight. After Paul's sight was restored, he spent time in Damascus with other followers of Christ. He grew in power and proclaimed the good news of Jesus. The conversion was complete. Paul had come to Damascus in order to persecute the followers of Christ, but God had different plans. On the way, Paul met Christ and became His follower. Before the conclusion of Acts 9, Paul, the one time persecutor of Christians, was forced to flee for his life because he was being persecuted for his faith.

God seems to enjoy using irony to make His power known. He chose the youngest of Jesse's sons to be the King of Israel.[353] He used a prostitute to save the lives of Jewish men.[354] He spoke to His people through a young boy instead of a respected priest.[355] In the New Testament, He chose to use a man who had been a sworn enemy of Christ's followers to proclaim the good news of Jesus around the world.

Conversion stories are wonderful reassurances to God's people that He is still working in this world. I love to read the accounts of those who have experienced an incredible transformation in their lives. God works in remarkably diverse ways to reveal Himself to those who are far away from Him.

Jon Kregel began following Christ when he faced a long prison sentence as a result of selling illegal drugs.[356] C.S. Lewis began to trust Christ after years of intellectually searching for answers to his perplexing questions.[357] Charles Colson experienced spiritual rebirth during a time when he faced serious legal consequences for his involvement in a presidential scandal.[358] Saint Augustine heard a voice tell him to pick up the Bible and read, and he believed.[359] Jolene DeHeer trusted in Christ as her Savior after seeing a vision.[360]

Each of these people, and many others, has experienced the life changing work of Jesus Christ. Each of these people has been used by God to advance His Kingdom. God takes delight in drawing people to Himself in many different ways. He can intellectually convince us that He is Lord. He can comfort us in our times of sorrow to convince us of His grace. He can appear to us miraculously. He can even stop us in our tracks, as we plan to hurt His church, and change our hearts.

Sought By Christ

How does faith start?

When people look back on their conversion experience, they almost always realize that their conversion was a result of God seeking them. They follow Christ because He first sought them and convinced them of His love.

Paul was not seeking God on his way to Damascus. He was seeking to destroy God's church. In the middle of this journey, God altered the course of his life. Christ spoke to Paul, not because Paul was seeking answers, but because Christ was seeking Paul.

Followers of Christ can be comforted by the knowledge that God worked in their lives before they committed themselves to following Him. He initiated the relationship. This is true for people who have wonderful stories of radical conversions as well as people who cannot remember a time when they did not know about Jesus.

People like Paul can look back at the moment in time when they first believed in Jesus. They can see that God worked in some way to bring them to faith in Him. The moments of their conversions were not the results of their own efforts to find God, but of God's efforts to find them. They follow Christ because they realize that Christ worked to make Himself known to them.

If you are a person who has a powerful conversion story, I hope that you can look back to see how God guided you into a loving relationship with Jesus. But even if you are a follower of Christ without a story of a mystical and radical conversion experience, you can still look back at your life and see that God was the one who initiated a loving relationship with you.

I am a person who does not have a story of a single, life changing moment. I do not remember the first time I believed that Jesus died for me. Like many other followers of Christ, I came to know about Jesus through my parents, who brought me to church every Sunday. I do not remember the first time I prayed to ask Jesus into my heart. I do not remember a day that I did not believe in Jesus.

My faith is not a result of my searching for God; it is a result of God working in my life before I was aware of His existence. He placed me in a family with Christian parents. He gave me a church home with loving people who taught me about Christ through Sunday School, boy's club, and youth group. I was blessed to attend a school with Christian teachers. These were blessings that God gave me. He sought me before I knew Him.

In Paul's letters to the churches in Rome and Ephesus, he mentions the idea of predestination.[361] When Paul says God predestined us, he is saying that God worked in our lives to redeem us before we were aware of His activity. Salvation is a gift from God, given to His chosen people. If you are a follower of Christ, it is because God chose to work in your life and opened your eyes to the wonderful gift of His Son, Jesus. You came to have faith in Christ because God drew you to Himself. Your act of following is a response to His initiative.

Predestination does not mean that God pre-determined each and every event that would occur in your life. He knows what events will transpire, but He does not cause each of those individual events to occur. If we believe that God causes each and every event to occur in our lives, then we have to say that God is responsible for sin, and God did not cause evil to enter this world. Sin and evil are the result of human rebellion.

Predestination means that no matter what may transpire, God is going to work out His plan to bring His chosen people into His eternal Kingdom. The events of this lifetime might be unsettling and disturbing, but your eternal destination is secure. If you are a Christian, God secured your destination before you knew the stories of His grace. If you are a follower of Christ, nothing can separate you from His love.[362]

The comfort of predestination is that God has worked tirelessly to secure your future. He is not going to let you fall away from Him. He is holding on to you.

Many followers try to read more into the teaching of predestination. They want to believe that God not only secures their eternal destiny, but also lays out a specified course in life for each of His followers. When Paul wrote about being predestined, he was speaking of God's wondrous work to secure his eternal future. He was not attempting to say that every step he took had been pre-determined by God.

God often does prescribe a specific course for individual followers. He called Moses to lead the people of Israel out of Egypt.[363] He called Gideon to lead Israel into battle against the Midianites.[364] He called Samuel to speak to His people.[365] However, not every follower of Christ receives such specific instructions for their lives. We are called to follow Christ. We should strive to discern God's leading. However, the fact that God predestines us for eternity with Him does not mean that every follower of Christ will have a daily prescribed course of specific actions from God. God's directions for our lives are often spelled out in broad terms. We are called to love Him with all of our strength and to love our neighbors.[366] We are told to walk with God.[367] We are not always clearly told where we should live, whom we should marry, what kind of career we should pursue, or what kind of vehicle we should drive.

Some people do receive specific leadings from God. Not only did God work to bring Paul into a saving relationship with Jesus, He had also chosen to use Paul as an instrument to spread the good news of Jesus.[368] God often worked to guide Paul on his missionary journeys. But even with God's guidance, Paul did not receive daily instructions.

At one point in his ministry, Paul wanted to move to an area called Bithynia. Somehow, God's Spirit prevented him from going there, and God sent Paul a dream. In that dream, Paul was called to alter his plans and go to Macedonia instead.[369] Paul's ministry was not a routine of following daily instructions, but a result of following Christ. Paul made efforts to glorify God, and was ready to listen when God wanted to alter his path.

This story is a wonderful lesson for followers of Christ. We can rest in the knowledge that God has predestined His children for eternity with Him. He also guides us today. We have freedom to seek His will. There are countless ways we can use our gifts to honor and praise Him. I believe that followers of Christ should seek God's will and then feel free to honor Him in the way they see fit. We can do this with the confidence of knowing that if He wants us to alter our plans; He can lead us as He led Paul.

No Second Class Followers

Despite Paul's background of persecuting the church, he was not considered an inferior follower of Christ. In fact, he was considered an apostle.[370] He was given the same status as Peter and John within the church, even though he had once persecuted the church.

The story of Paul's conversion stands as a shining example of what God can do in a person's life. God can turn a person completely around. Someone who was once Christ's enemy can be transformed into an instrument to bring glory to God.

Christ's forgiveness removes the stain and shame of sin. Paul was not considered a second class Christian. Even though some of his fellow believers were initially skeptical about his conversion,[371] once they realized what God had done in his life, they welcomed him into their fellowship.

Followers of Christ are called to welcome fellow believers into their fellowship. We do not carry grudges nor withhold friendship due to sins of the past. When Christ offers forgiveness, His followers welcome that person as though she had never sinned. All of Christ's followers are full members of His body despite the history of sin in their lives.

Paul was keenly aware of his past sins, but he was also aware that the sins of his past did not lessen the value of God's work in his life. In his letters, Paul referred to himself as the least of the apostles because he had been abnormally born.[372] He acknowledged his sin, and expressed proper remorse. However, he also boldly proclaimed that he was not inferior to other apostles.[373]

Paul's life is an uplifting example for Christians who struggle with the guilt of their past sins. We have all been guilty of sins, and we should not take our sins lightly. The sins of our past should remind us that we need the grace of Christ. We should not speak of our sins with an air of nostalgia or a sense of pride. We can acknowledge our guilt with humility. Yet at the same time we can be grateful for the way God works in our lives, and we can follow Christ without apologizing for the direction He leads us. We might even find that we enjoy the work God has done through us. We will find moments that we are pleased with the way God has used us. Despite the sins of our past, we may also find moments to boast in the Lord for what He has done.[374]

Christ's Work Continues

In Paul's life, we see the Gospel of Jesus Christ moving beyond the first generation. In his life, we see signs that the movement of Jesus was not going to die with those who knew Him before His crucifixion.

With any organized movement, there is a fear that the movement will cease once the original members cease to exercise an active role. Nations, businesses, and non-profit organizations work diligently to lay a foundation of rules so that their organizations will continue to thrive for an indefinite period of time.

The early church may have feared the loss of its original leaders. What would happen to this movement once Peter, James, and John died? Would the followers of Christ continue to thrive as a community?

In the beginning of Acts, the leaders of the church were the people who had known Jesus throughout His earthly ministry. When Peter and the other disciples were looking for someone to replace Judas Iscariot, they narrowed their search by only considering people who had been with Jesus throughout His earthly ministry.[375]

As the church grew, so did the number of leaders. It was impossible for the original apostles to minister to the entire church. They recruited other leaders.[376] Presumably, some of those leaders had not followed Christ throughout His earthly ministry.

Once Paul became a leader in the church, the church could see signs that this movement was not going to falter. Even though Peter and John would eventually die, God would continue to raise new leaders. His church would not fail.

Since Christ's resurrection, nations have risen and fallen. Businesses have been started and closed. But the movement of Christ continues. God continues to bring forth leaders for His people.

I often hear people worrying about the future of the Church. I do not worry. Even though I regularly see things in our world that cause me concern, I do not fear the church will die. I am confident that the God who established His church through the blood of Jesus Christ, who worked through men like Peter and John, and who continued His work through men like Paul will also continue the movement through our troubled times. I do not know how God will continue His church. I am not confident that every denomination that exists today will continue to exist. Neither am I confident that every individual congregation will thrive in ministry. However, I am sure that God will continue the work of proclaiming the good news of Jesus, and I am confident that He will continue to care for Christ's followers.

Questions for discussion/reflection:

How did God work in your life before you ever knew you needed Him? Who are some people He used to guide you?

Does predestination mean that God prescribes every detail of our lives?

How can past sins hinder our ability to effectively serve Christ? What does the story of Paul teach us about this?

Do you ever worry that the Church is going to lose its effectiveness? How does God's work in Paul's life reassure you that God will continue to sustain His followers?

Chapter 15
The Unheralded Crowd

Offensive linemen are probably the most unheralded players in the NFL. Sports reporters will often applaud the efforts of quarterbacks and running backs. Defensive players are frequently praised for their skill and tenacity, but you almost never hear about offensive linemen. They have a tough job. They are given the task of keeping defensive players away from their quarterback and opening lanes for their running back. The quarterbacks and running backs will find their names in the paper for their efforts, but you will only hear about the offensive linemen when they make mistakes.

Offensive linemen understand that they are not playing for personal glory. If they wanted to see their names in the headlines, they should have played a different sport. Yet, despite the lack of personal recognition, offensive linemen can occasionally find glory as part of a team. When a running back breaks a record for yards gained, the offensive linemen rightly consider themselves a part of that record. When a football team wins the Superbowl, their offensive line played a crucial role in their victory, even if you do not know their names.

Unheralded Disciples

Very few followers of Christ will receive recognition from humans for their role in God's plans. Most Christians have heard stories of Peter and Paul. We know the names of Old Testament characters like David, Moses, Abraham, and Noah. We might even be familiar with contemporary leaders in God's Church. However, most followers of Christ will go largely unheralded. Most followers of Christ are like offensive linemen in the NFL. They might play an important role in His Kingdom, but they are not playing for their own personal glory.

Followers of Christ seek God's glory. He called us to be His children so that we could glorify Him.[377] When God is glorified, we are pleased. That glory reflects on us.

Many of the original twelve disciples receive little or no mention in the Bible after Christ's ascension. We do not know what happened to them. I think it would be interesting to know what occurred in the lives of these followers after Christ ascended. What happened to Philip after the conversion of the Ethiopian?[378] Did Thomas ever go on a missionary journey? Why was it so important to tell us that Matthias became an apostle, when the Bible never records his name following his selection?[379] There are traditions and legends about some of the twelve original apostles, but most of them are never mentioned after Acts 1. Their names fade into the background.

The lack of personal notoriety does not mean that the work of the original twelve disciples was meaningless. The fact that Christ's church still exists today is a testimony to the way God used those twelve men.

In roughly two thousand years of church history, there have been countless numbers of church leaders. Most of the names of these leaders are not remembered today. When asked to name historical leaders in the Christian Church, most Christians might recall the names of Saint Augustine, Martin Luther, and one or two popes. We do not have many Christian leaders whose names are heralded. This does not mean that their efforts are unappreciated. These people did not live to bring themselves glory, but to bring glory to God. Because of their efforts, God has been glorified.[380]

Followers of Christ do not seek praise from other humans.[381] We want to please God and direct others to praise Him. The early disciples, who are hardly mentioned after Acts 1, remind us that there will be many followers who do not achieve the status of being well-known by others. But they can still be used and honored by God. They will share in His eternal inheritance.

The Death of James

During Christ's ministry, Peter, James, and John seemed to be the three disciples that were closest to Him. They witnessed the transfiguration. Christ only allowed these three to follow Him when he healed the daughter of a synagogue ruler.[382] James was part of the inner circle of Christ's disciples. His insights and experience could have been very useful for the early church.

Sadly, James was put to death by those who opposed the Christian faith.[383] He was taken prisoner by Herod, and subsequently executed.

James' death received remarkably little attention in the New Testament. One would think that the author of Acts would have taken time to tell the story of James' life when his death was mentioned. But the story of James' death is not a central story. In fact, it seems to be part of an explanation for why Peter was arrested.

James' death reminds us that followers of Christ are not promised earthly success. Even though James had been a faithful follower, his life was taken. In our human nature, we might want to argue with God over the death of James. We might reason that James could have been so useful for God's Kingdom that he should not have suffered the tragedy of death. We might observe that his death was probably a traumatic event in the lives of the other original disciples. In our boldness, we could argue that it would have been wise for God to intervene and spare James from his untimely death.

I must confess that when things don't go well in my life, I often begin a debate with God. I want to know why God allows terrible things to happen. Even though I trust that God is good and powerful, I wonder why He allows certain events to transpire. Why does He allow me to act foolishly? Why doesn't He give me clearer guidance? Why doesn't He make serving Him a little more convenient? When I read the story of James, I am forced to see that God has a plan that is bigger than making my life convenient.

As we struggle with questions about suffering, we can be reassured that even though suffering is real, God continues to advance His plans. Our weeping may endure for a long period of time that seems very dark, but God will bring the joy of morning to our lives.[384] The success of

God's church in the face of James' death teaches us that God's Kingdom plans will not be stopped by evil.

The death of James reminds us that the advancement of God's Kingdom does not rely on any individual, no matter how gifted or influential he might be. Despite the loss of one of the prominent leaders, Christ's church continued to grow. New leaders in the church were raised by God to continue His ministry. James' death may have been a loss to the church, but God's church was going to continue.

Followers of Christ often succumb to the idea that they are carrying the weight of the world on their shoulders. We are part of something important when we follow Christ. We can easily develop the mindset that the work we do as individuals is so significant that if we were to quit, the entire Kingdom movement might be damaged.

The story of James' death is simultaneously humbling and comforting. It is humbling, because it demonstrates that Christ's work can thrive even with the loss of someone as prominent as James. Our efforts can be fruitful for God's plans, but none of our efforts are indispensable to His Kingdom. This story is also comforting, because it takes a load of worry off of our shoulders. We are not responsible to bring the fullness of Christ's Kingdom. We are called to follow Christ. We submit to God's commandments for our lives. We give our best effort for Him. But even if we cannot perform perfectly, He will still bring His plans to completion.

The advancement of the good news of Jesus Christ is larger than any individual follower. God can continue His work even in the face of a tragic loss. The death of James reminds us that even faithful followers are subject to suffer evil in this world. Yet evil will not prevail. God's word continues to move forward. Even though James died, Christ's followers continued to grow in numbers. Christ continued to receive praise.

James does not receive the recognition that Peter and John receive. Yet God used His life and continues to advance His Kingdom. James may have been an unheralded offensive lineman in God's church, but His efforts were used by God to glorify Christ.

What About the Others?

The Bible does not record the death of any of the other original apostles. We only hear about James, and we do not hear too many details about his experience. My curiosity causes me to wonder what happened to the others. We do not hear too much about them.

In Acts 1, the Bible records the names of the twelve disciples, including Matthias, who replaced Judas Iscariot. After that chapter, the names of Andrew, Thomas, Bartholomew, Matthew, James the son of Alpheus, Simon the Zealot, Judas the son of James, and Matthias are never mentioned again. What happened in the lives of these eight apostles? There are legends and historical traditions that give us a little information about their ministry, but there are not a lot of details. The Bible does not tell us where they went on missionary journeys. We do not know how they died. The stories of their lives seem to be lost. However, the lack of stories is no indication that their lives were not useful for God's Kingdom. Their efforts were used to bring glory to God. They may be unheralded, but they were not working for the praise of other humans. Their efforts were intended to honor Christ.

Even though Peter, John, and Philip are mentioned after Acts 1, we do not know a great deal about the ends of their lives. We read about Philip preaching in Samaria and baptizing an Ethiopian eunuch, but the last thing the Bible tells us about him is that he traveled around proclaiming the gospel from Azotus to Caesarea.[385] The Bible tells us that Peter was miraculously rescued from prison,[386] but after that he is only mentioned one more time in the book of Acts.[387] Tradition tells us that Peter was eventually crucified for his faith. His last request was to be crucified upside down, because he believed himself unworthy of being executed in the same manner as Jesus. The book of Revelation is the last Biblical record of John's life. He was apparently exiled to an island, where he wrote the final book of the Bible.

Paul's life story follows a similar pattern in the Bible. We know that he went on many missionary trips, and that he hoped to travel to Rome. In the book of Acts, we last witness him en route to Rome, where he was to be put on trial. Today, many people travel to Rome to view the cell where it is believed Paul spent his last days, writing many letters to followers of Christ around the world. But the Bible never tells us how Paul's life ended.

Even though these men all played significant roles in the early Christian Church, we hear very little about the end of their lives. We do not hear about the end of their lives, because their deaths are not the significant stories of God's early church. The fact that these men died is not crucial to the story of God's work. The stories of their deaths may be interesting, but they should in no way overshadow the story of the one death that does concern us: the death of Jesus. His death is the crucial death in the Bible's story. Other deaths pale in comparison. Other deaths do not warrant mentioning in God's word, because those deaths do not take away from the power of God's ongoing work. Because of Jesus' death and resurrection, the deaths of His followers are not the final story of His Kingdom. Jesus' work continues even when His followers lose their lives. Their lives become part of the greater work of bringing honor and praise to Christ.

Fading into the Background

Followers of Christ are not seeking personal glory. They are seeking glory for their Leader. If the stories of our lives fade into obscurity while the Kingdom of Christ flourishes, we rejoice. We are grateful that we can be utilized by God to advance His plans.

I must confess that it is nice to receive praise from other people. Encouraging words can lift a person's spirits. The acknowledgment of our efforts can encourage us to continue serving our Lord. However, we do not live for the praise of other people. We should not expect every one of our efforts to be noticed. In fact, some of the greatest blessings are the humble acts of service that often go virtually unnoticed by others.

After washing their feet, Jesus told His followers that they should submit to each other in humility.[388] Following Christ is not a process of seeking glory. Instead, it is a process that involves seeking opportunities to serve others. It calls us to let go of our hopes that we will be recognized for our efforts, so that Christ can be recognized for His grace.

I am amazed by Christ's followers today. Despite the self-centered nature of our world, I still see many of Christ's followers striving to serve God and others without demanding recognition. Some faithful followers even shy away from any kind of recognition.

I have been blessed to be part of a church family that is comprised of many people who willingly fade into the background so that Christ can be praised. Occasionally, I will hear stories of what God's people will do without asking for recognition.

Jan has been known to enter the home of someone who is sick in order to clean house and do the laundry. No one asked her to do it. She never asked for recognition. She followed Christ's example of serving.

Dan and Wanda will recruit a group of young people to help them do yard work for someone who is hurting.

Every spring, Gerald and Henrietta will go to the home of a widow in our church to install the screens in her windows.

Tress and Sylvia regularly meet in church to decorate the sanctuary for the holiday worship services.

Whenever Elaine notices that someone is sick, she calls others from church to coordinate a schedule for bringing meals.

Paul, Bart, and Dick will notice when something is need of repair within church and fix it before most people notice it was ever broken.

Dee created a ministry of friendship by calling people on the phone and asking them how they were doing.

Bernie and Anna would regularly plan and prepare a meal for those who attended the funeral of a loved one.

Jerry will give children a ride on the motorized cart he uses to come into church.

Todd and Shelly have an open door to their house. If anyone wants to come over to talk, or to live for a few months, they are ready to welcome them.

These are just a few examples in one church of some of the things that people have done to serve God. They do this without seeking recognition. In fact, some of them will be a little perturbed with me for using their names. They would not think of themselves as charismatic leaders, but through their work, they are ministering to others and setting an example of faithfully following Christ that others will imitate.

I am thankful for their efforts. They each work to glorify God in some way. They willingly serve, not so that other people will take notice of their good deeds, but so that God will be glorified. They willingly take on the role of offensive linemen in the church. Their efforts often go unheralded, but the effect of their work has brought blessings to others that they might not even be aware of.

Followers of Christ will often go without the recognition of other people. However, their labor in the lord is not in vain.[389] God often uses the acts that go unnoticed by human eyes to bring His blessings. When we relinquish the pursuit of our own personal recognition, our actions can be used to help others recognize God.

Questions for discussion/reflection:
Why doesn't the Bible record what happened to most of the original disciples after Acts 1?

Does following Christ guarantee success and notoriety in this lifetime? Explain.

What kind of success does God really promise? Is it possible for us to have God's success and still experience periodic struggles?

Think of some people you admire for the way they model Christ-likeness? Do most of them receive accolades? If not, what value is their service?

Chapter 16
Catch the Vision

Have you ever watched television very early on a Sunday morning? Many stations take a break from regular programming, and fill the airwaves with thirty minute advertisements called "infomercials." As I flip through the channels on my television, I cannot help being drawn into these strange programs. They all offer something that would be helpful to a wide target audience such as programs for making money in real estate, exercise equipment or diet pills that will reshape your body, facial creams that will remove blemishes and bring a youthful appearance, or kitchen appliances that will simplify meal preparation.

All of these infomercial products have one characteristic in common: they offer a quick-fix to a common problem. People who want more money can quickly accumulate wealth. Those who struggle with their body image can lose weight or have firmer skin in a relatively short period of time—and without much effort. If you wish you could spend less time in the kitchen, you merely have to buy the latest time-saving device.

I like to save time as much as anyone and I must confess that I get impatient whenever I have to wait in line at a store, or wait on hold for operator assistance. When I have a problem, I want it resolved as soon as possible. However, when my desire for quick resolution seeps into my walk with Christ, I am setting myself up for frustration.

The Quick Fix

Faith in Christ is not a quick-fix to our temporary troubles.

I must confess that there have been times in my life when I was under the false impression that I was able to catch Christ. In other words, I thought I could pray the right way, read the right scripture passages, and sing the right songs that would make Jesus fix the problems that were on my mind. I knew the stories of God miraculously parting the waters of the Red Sea[390] and I thought that if I trusted Him enough, He would clear every hindrance to my plans. I thought the Christian life was a quick-fix to my problems, and that by "catching Christ" I could find the key to solving my dilemmas. I wrongly assumed that once I followed Christ for a sufficient period of time, I would be able to take over the reigns of my life and make Him perform my will.

Instead, I discovered that Christ is not always interested in solving my immediate dilemmas. Following Him is not a quick-fix to my problems, but rather it is a process by which I am changed. I do not "catch" Christ, but rather, He "catches" me. As I pursue Jesus, He gradually changes my will and my desires so that the things I want "fixed" do not seem so significant. My pursuit of Jesus changes me, rather than changing the immediate problems I face. I have found that even when God does intervene in order to "fix" my problems; it usually serves a greater purpose of changing me by strengthening faith or reassuring me of His presence.

In the summer of 1994, I led a group of high school students on a bike trip across the state of Michigan. During one of our breaks, one of the riders lost her contact lens. She had been standing and walking alongside the road in very tall grass when her contact lens fell, and my first thought was that we would never find that contact lens again. I was somewhat skeptical when the rider asked her friend to pray that they would be able to find the contact lens in the tall grass along the roadside. As I watched them bow their heads and pray, I wondered how we could help this rider navigate the rest of the bike trip with only one good eye. My worries were immediately proven worthless when a series of events unfolded before my eyes.

After the girls completed their prayer with "amen," one of them looked down, and while the sound of the prayer was still echoing in my ears, she screamed in an elated voice, "I see it!" She reached her hand to touch a clump of grass, and pulled it up with the contact lens balanced on the end of her index finger. I was struck by how quickly the girls found the contact lens once they completed their prayer. I was immediately convinced that this was not a mere coincidence.

For the first few hours following that answered prayer, I felt a mixture of emotions. On the one hand, I was glad that the rider found her contact lens. On the other hand, it seemed like a wasted prayer. If God was going to answer a prayer, I would have preferred He heal someone who was chronically ill, or freed someone from an oppressive situation. I wondered why God would take the time to answer a seemingly insignificant prayer request when there were significant problems in the world.

It didn't take me long to understand what God was doing. By that evening of the bike trip, every student had heard the story of the answered prayer, and all were struck by how God was working on that trip. The members of that biking group developed a sense of expectation when they prayed. They believed that God was revealing His power in them. That bike became one of the best youth ministry experiences I ever had the pleasure of leading. Lives were transformed.

I am not so sure that God is too concerned about contact lenses, but I am confident that He is interested in the faith of His children. On that bike trip, He answered a prayer for a contact lens that ended up setting a tone for the trip that had a long term effect on many young people. It seemed as though God offered a "quick-fix" to a minor problem, when in fact, He was shaping a group of young people to expect Him to act in their lives.

God can miraculously bring instant relief to our lives, and sometimes He does. However, God does not promise that every problem we face will have a quick and easy solution because we trust Jesus. God does not promise a quick-fix, but He does welcome us into a lifelong journey.

Being Caught by the Vision

When I first became serious about my faith, I was under the impression that I could make myself into a dynamic tool that God could use. I believed that my walk with God could mirror the development of a great athlete. I would train hard, learn God's Word, volunteer for the right Christian agencies, and God would make great things happen because of my efforts. In a way, I believed that my effort would cause me to catch God. I imagined myself being filled with His spiritual gifts and becoming so holy that God would be compelled to answer my prayers and work in my life. I believed my efforts would captivate God. In other words, I thought that I could "catch" Jesus, much like I have been catching my sons in the games I have played with them over the past few years.

Don't misunderstand me. I have truly wanted God to be glorified, and I have sincerely prayed that His will would be done in my life. I was merely under the impression that His will would best be done once I trained myself into being a "super Christian" and started using my finely-tuned skills for Him.

But something surprising has happened in the process. I have discovered that I will never "catch" Christ; and I am learning that even though God loves me, my giftedness will never captivate Him. Instead, as I strive to follow Christ, I find that I am captivated by what Jesus has done for me and what His Holy Spirit continues to do in me. I am learning that in the process of following, I have been overwhelmed by Christ's plan for me. I have been changed from thinking that I could do God a favor by serving Him into realizing that He has given me great joy as I lose sight of my plans and see His plan unfolding for me. To be honest, there are times when God's plan is nothing like what I had planned for myself. Sometimes, I even struggle as I follow Him. But God has given me great joy and peace as I look to Him.

When I play with my children, I care very little whether I win or lose the game we are playing. I enjoy the process of getting to know them through the game we play. Similarly, as I follow Christ, I am learning that the joy is not found in the development of my ability to follow, but in the fact that He captivates my attention.

When you give someone your attention, you give them the ability to change you. This is true of television. As you watch TV, you are influenced by commercials that seek to change your buying habits. This is also true of friends. As you spend time with people you admire, you begin to adapt their likes and dislikes, and you may even imitate their mannerisms and expressions. Similarly, when your attention is captivated by Christ, you are giving Him the ability to transform you. In reality, as we follow Him, and even try to catch Him, He ends up catching us and making us new. A life spent following Christ is a dynamic journey of discovering what God has planned for you.

Sent Out

Throughout most of the gospels, Jesus' followers were called "disciples." They were students who were fully devoted to Him. They followed where He led, even if they did not understand. They were in the process of being changed. Since they were students, they were being prepared for a mission.

People who serve in the military are required to endure a time of basic training.[391] In this time, they learn the skills that are necessary to be an effective soldier. They learn to reflexively obey the orders of their superiors. They learn to identify themselves by their association with their unit.

Basic training is a necessary time, but men and women are not received into the military for the purpose of enduring basic training. They endure basic training to be prepared for a mission.

Jesus' plan of discipleship was not merely to cause His disciples to endure traveling with Him around the Middle East. He was preparing them for a mission. His method of teaching His followers was an intentional effort to train them for His purposes.[392]

Jesus began His ministry by telling His disciples to follow. They came and they watched as He performed miracles. He turned water into wine.[393] He healed incurable ailments.[394] The disciples listened as he traveled and taught.

Jesus then called His disciples to help Him in His ministry. When the crowds were hungry, Jesus told His disciples to give them something to eat.[395] After He divided the food, the disciples were involved in distributing it to the crowds. They had grown from observers of His ministry to participants in His work.

The disciples continued to grow in their training as Jesus sent them out on their own to teach, cast out demons, and heal the sick.[396] Even though they had started as mere observers, Christ was giving them authority, and they experienced success in their efforts.

Once the disciples were sent out to follow Christ's instruction, they were given a new title. They were called apostles. Apostle means sent out. Jesus had called these people to follow Him so that they could be trained to do His will. They were given the task to complete His mission. They had started as students who were learning from their teacher. But once they had learned through experience, Christ sent them out on their own.

After Christ's ascension, the book of Acts refers to His original twelve followers as apostles. Their basic training was complete, and they had received their mission orders. They were called to go out into the world, and make new disciples.[397] They were still following Jesus. They were obeying His commands and they were being led by His Holy Spirit. However, following had taken them from the status of student, or disciple, and transformed them into people who were ready to be sent out with their mission orders.

Following the Leader will call you to a life of participating in Christ's Kingdom plans. He will move you from an observer, to a participant, to a recipient of mission orders. He will give you the resources and the strength you need, because He is still leading His mission. This is His battle for your sake, and He will bring His plans to completion. He has a plan to prosper you and give you His peace.[398] He will transform you into what He intends you to be.[399] You will be given an assignment as you walk with Him into the fullness of His Kingdom.

Follow Him.

Questions for discussion/reflection:
What kind of "quick fixes" do people often look for when the turn to God in prayer?

Does transformation mean that we become more pleasing to God, or that God becomes more satisfying to us?

How has Christ been training you for service? Have you experienced spiritual growth as you have tried to honor Him with your service? Explain.

What is the relationship between being a student of Christ and being sent out for Christ?

Bibliography

Adsit, Christopher B. Personal Disciplemaking: A Step-by-step Guide for Leading a Christian From New Birth to Maturity. Here's Life Publishers, Inc. SanBernadino, CA. 1988.

Augustine, Saint. Confessions. Translated by Henry Chadwick. Oxford University Press. New York, NY. 1992.

Barth, Karl. The Call to Discipleship. Excerpt from Church Dogmatics (volume 4, part 2) Translated by G.W. Bromiley. Edited by K.C. Hanson. Fortress Press. Minneapolis, MN. 2003.

Bonhoeffer, Dietrich. The Cost of Discipleship. Translated by Chr. Kaiser Verlag Munchen by R.H. Fuller, with some revision by Irmgard Booth. Touchstone. New York, NY. 1995.

Borg, Marcus. Editor. Jesus and Buddha: The Parallel Sayings. Seastone. Berkeley, CA.1997.

Bright, Bill. Witnessing Without Fear: How to Share Your Faith With Confidence. Here's Life Publishers, Inc. San Bernadino, CA. 1987.

Chambers, Oswald. My Utmost For His Highest: An Updated Edition In Today's Language. Edited by James Reimann. Discovery House Publishers. Grand Rapids, MI. 1992

Clinton, Dr. J. Robert. The Making of a Leader. NavPress. Colorado Springs, CO. 1988.

Coleman, Robert E. The Master Plan of Evangelism. Thirtieth Anniversary Edition. Fleming H. Revell. Grand Rapids, MI. 1993.

Colson, Charles W. Born Again. Twentieth Anniversary Edition. Fleming H. Revell. Grand Rapids, MI. 1997.

Colson, Charles. Loving God. Zondervan Publishing House. Grand Rapids, MI. 1983.

Couperus, Sid. "Becoming a Fully Devoted Disciple of Jesus." The

Banner. March, 2004. Volume 139. Number 3. Pages 28-30.

Culpepper, R. Allen. Anatomy of the Fourth Gospel: A Study In Literary Design. Fortress Press. Philadelphia, PA. 1983.

Edwards, Jonathan. The Religious Affections. The Banner of Truth Trust. Carlisle, PA. First Published: 1746. First Banner of Truth Edition: 1961. Reprinted: 1994.

Foster, Richard J. Celebration of Discipline: The Path to Spiritual Growth. Twentieth Anniversary Edition. Harper SanFrancisco. SanFrancisco, CA. 1998.

Hansel, Tim. Holy Sweat. Word Publishing. Dallas, TX. 1987.

Hybels, Bill. Honest To God? Becoming an Authentic Christian. Guideposts. Carmel, NY. 1990.

Hybels, Bill. Too Busy Not To Pray: Slowing Down to Be With God. Tenth Anniversary Edition. Intervarsity Press. Downers Grove, IL. 1998.

Jones, Laurie Beth. Jesus CEO: Using Ancient Wisdom for Visionary Leadership. Hyperion. New York, NY. 1995.

Kempis, Thomas 'a. The Imitation of Christ. Edited and Translated by Joseph N. Tylenda, S.J. Vintage Books. New York, NY. 1998.

Kregel, Jon. Dealer: A Soccer Pro's Deliverance from the Cocaine Underworld. Kregel Publications. Grand Rapids, MI. 1998.

Lawrence, Brother. The Practice of the Presence of God. Translated by John J. Delaney. An Image Book Published by Doubleday. New York, NY. 1977.

Lewis, C.S. Mere Christianity. MacMillan Publishing Company. New York, NY. 1943, 1945, 1952.

Lewis, C.S. The Screwtape Letters. MacMillan Company, Inc. New York, NY. 1976.

Lewis, C.S. Surprised By Joy: The Shape Of My Early Life. Harcourt Brace and Company. Orlando, FL. 1956, 1984.

Ortberg, John. If You Want to Walk on Water, You've Got to Get out of the Boat. Zondervan, Grand Rapids, MI. 2001.

Ortberg, John. The Life You've Always Wanted: Spiritual Disciplines for Ordinary People. Zondervan. Grand Rapids, MI. 1997.

Ortberg, John. Love Beyond Reason: Moving God's Love from Your

Head to Your Heart. Zondervan Publishing House. Grand Rapids, MI. 1998.

Peterson, Eugene H. Subversive Spirituality. William B. Eerdmans Publishing Company. Grand Rapids, MI. 1994.

Plantinga, Cornelius Jr. "Hypocrisy and Grace: A Meditation for Lent." The Banner. February, 2004. Volume 39. Number 2. Pages 40-42.

Plantinga, Cornelius Jr. Not The Way It's Supposed to Be: A Breviary of Sin. Wm. B. Eerdmans Publishing Co. Grand Rapids, MI. 1995.

Smedes, Lewis B. Union With Christ. Revised Edition. William B. Eerdmans Publishing Co. 1983.

Stott, John R.W. Basic Christianity. Second Edition. Intervarsity Press. Downers Grove, IL. 1971.

Strobel, Lee. The Case For Christ: A Journalist's Personal Investigation of the Evidence for Jesus. Zondervan Publishing House. Grand Rapids, MI. 1998.

Strobel, Lee. The Case For Faith: A Journalist Investigates the Toughest Objections to Christianity. Zondervan Publishing House. Grand Rapids, MI. 2000.

Tozer, A.W. The Pursuit of God: The Human Thirst for the Divine. Christian Publications, Inc. Camp Hill, PA. 1982, 1993.

Wagner, E. Glenn. Escape from Church, Inc: The Return of the Pastor-Shepherd. Zondervan Publishing House. Grand Rapids, MI. 1999.

Warren, Rick. The Purpose Driven Life: What On Earth Am I Here For? Zondervan. Grand Rapids, MI. 2002.

Wenham, Gordon J. The Book of Leviticus. The New International Commentary on the Old Testament. William B. Eerdmans Publishing Company. 1979.

Willard, Dallas. Hearing God. InterVarsity Press. Downers Grove, IL. 1984. Reprinted: 1993.

Willard, Dallas. The Spirit of the Disciplines: Understanding How God Changes Lives. Harper San Francisco. San Francisco, CA. 1988.

Willimon, William H. Pastor: The Theology and Practice of Ordained Ministry. Abingdon Press. Nashville, TN. 2002.

Woodward, Kenneth L. "The Other Jesus." Newsweek. March 27, 2000. Volume CXXXV. Number 13. Pages 50-60.

Wright, H. Norman. Simplify Your Life and Get More Out of It! Tyndale House Publishers, Inc. Wheaton, IL. 1998.

Yancey, Philip. The Jesus I Never Knew. Zondervan Publishing House. Grand Rapids, MI. 1995.

Yancey, Philip. Reaching for the Invisible God: What Can We Expect to Find? Zondervan Publishing House. Grand Rapids, MI. 2000.

Yancey, Philip. What's So Amazing About Grace? Zondervan Publishing House. Grand Rapids, MI. 1997

Young, Brad H. Jesus The Jewish Theologian. Hendrickson Publishers. Peabody, MA. 1995.

Zacharias, Ravi. Jesus Among Other Gods: The Absolute Claims of the Christian Message. W Publishing Group. Nashville, TN. 2000.

Endnotes

Chapter 1
[1] John 3:3-7
[2] Mark 1:17
[3] Ephesians 6:10-17
[4] John 13:12-17
[5] 1 Corinthians 12
[6] Galatians 5:22-26
[7] Matthew 4:19, John 21:22
[8] Acts 16:31
[9] Romans 3:28
[10] 1 Peter 1:13
[11] James 2:24
[12] Matthew 4:19, Mark 1:16, Luke 5:27, John 1:43
[13] Luke 9:57-62
[14] Matthew 28:19
[15] Adsit, Christopher. Personal Disciplemaking. Pages 28-29. Adsit points out that the main verb of Christ's command is to make disciples. The other verbs—go, baptize, and teach—are all verbs that describe the circumstances for making disciples.

Chapter 2
[16] Matthew 18:21-35. In this parable not only do we learn about God, but we also learn that He wants us to imitate Him in by forgiving others.
[17] Luke 15:11-32.
[18] Matthew 22:1-14.
[19] Barth, Karl. The Call to Discipleship. Page 1.

[20] Kregel, Jon. Dealer.
[21] John 14:6
[22] I owe this phrase to Dr. Michael Williams, professor of Old Testament Studies at Calvin Theological Seminary.
[23] Ephesians 4:22-24
[24] Edwards, Jonathan. The Religious Affections.
[25] This story is told with Jolene's permission.
[26] Jolene DeHeer Ministries. www.jolenedeheer.com
[27] Exodus 3
[28] Luke 1:26-38
[29] 1 Samuel 3
[30] Acts 9
[31] Acts 16:31
[32] James 2:19
[33] James 2:17
[34] James 1:27

Chapter 3

[35] Woodward, Kenneth L. "The Other Jesus." Newsweek. March 27, 2000. Volume CXXXV. Number 13. Pages 50-60.
[36] A likeness of Jesus appeared on the March 27, 2000, issue of Newsweek magazine. A picture of an actor (James Caviezel) portraying Jesus appeared again on the cover of the February 16, 2004, issue. On the cover of the July 16, 2001, issue was the picture of a group of young people who were attending a Christian concert with the words, "Jesus Rocks." On the May 6, 2002, issue appeared the words, "What Would Jesus Do?" On the November 4, 2002, issue there was a cover story, "The Jesus Mystery." Only President George W. Bush made more cover appearances in that period of time.
[37] Matthew 28:18.
[38] Mark 1:22
[39] John 3:31-47
[40] "Chutzpah" is a Hebrew term that is difficult to define. In His book, Jesus the Jewish Theologian, Brad Young says that chutzpah "means headstrong persistence, brazen impudence, unyielding tenacity, bold

determination, or what in current English terms might be referred to as raw nerve." Page 171.
[41] John 6:15.
[42] Matthew 26:50-56.
[43] 1 Kings 18:20-40
[44] Matthew 8:7
[45] Luke 5:24
[46] Mark 4:39
[47] Matthew 9:1-3
[48] Stott, John R.W. Basic Christianity. Pages 23-26. Stott's reflection on Christ's teaching was foundational for this section.
[49] Borg, Marcus. Editor. Jesus and Buddha.
[50] Borg, Marcus. Editor. Jesus and Buddha. Pages xi-xii.
[51] John 14:6
[52] John 6:35
[53] John 8:12
[54] John 10:11-14
[55] John 13:13
[56] John 8:58. In this claim, Jesus is not only saying He lived before Abraham. He is also using the same words God used to identify Himself to Moses in Exodus 3:14-15. The Jews mentioned in John 8 understood Christ's claim in taking the name of God upon Himself, and that is why they prepared to stone Him in verse 59.
[57] Luke 9:57-62
[58] Matthew 16:21
[59] Luke 22:42
[60] John 18:1-11
[61] Colson, Charles. Loving God. Pages 61-70.
[62] I owe this point to C.S. Lewis. In His book, Mere Christianity Lewis points out that Christ does not give us the option of considering Him a good teacher. We must either submit to Him as Lord or consider Him a madman. Pages 51-56.

Chapter 4

[63] I owe thanks to my brother, Bob Sytsma, for this illustration. He ran the Chicago Marathon in October, 2002, and completed it in 4 hours, 13 minutes, and 42 seconds.
[64] Philippians 3:12-14.
[65] 2 Corinthians 5:17
[66] John 14:1-6.
[67] John 14:23
[68] Genesis 2:19
[69] Genesis 2:15
[70] Genesis 3:16
[71] John 15:18-25
[72] James 1:2-18
[73] John 9
[74] Job 42:7
[75] Psalm 1:3
[76] In his book, The Purpose Driven Life, Rick Warren compares new Christians to babies in a crib. When parents first bring home a new baby, they respond to every little cry. In doing this, parents give their children a sense of reassurance that they are present. However, good parents will eventually wean their children from that dependency. Warren suggests that God may be very attentive at first in order to reassure us of His presence. He may then gradually wean us from the dependency of seeing every prayer request answered immediately and directly so that we will mature. Page 109.
[77] James 1:2
[78] Matthew 11:30
[79] Proverbs 3:5-6
[80] Jesus gave this command 22 times in the gospels, and it occurs in each of the 4 gospels.
[81] Jesus gave this command 18 times in he gospels. It, too, occurs in each of the 4 gospels.
[82] This occurs too many times to count. For examples see Genesis 17:1, Genesis 5:21-24, Micah 6:8, Psalm 56:13.
[83] Matthew 22:37
[84] Matthew 14:22-36

[85] In his book, If You Want To Walk On Water, You've Got To Get Out Of The Boat, John Ortberg wonderfully describes the faith of Peter and clearly presents the implications of this story for our faith today.
[86] 1 Thessalonians 5:17
[87] I have borrowed this phrase from Philip Yancey's book, Reaching for the Invisible God. In Chapter 16 he asserts that it is all-to-easy for us to neglect God and to stop pursuing Him. Pages 197-208.
[88] Luke 17:6
[89] Matthew 22:37
[90] 2 Corinthians 4:18
[91] Hebrews 12:2
[92] Psalm 25:10
[93] Deuteronomy 31:6
[94] Proverbs 3:5-6
[95] In Deuteronomy 6, God instructed the people of Israel to bind His law on their wrists and on the doorways of their homes. They had to consider His will even in the food they ate and the way that they washed themselves. These practices turned their attention to Him.
[96] This list borrows heavily from Richard Foster's book, Celebration of Discipline: The Path to Spiritual Growth.
[97] Some of my favorite books include: The Life You've Always Wanted by John Ortberg; Too Busy Not To Pray by Bill Hybels; Simplify Your Life and Get More Out Of It! by H. Norman Wright; The Pursuit of God by A.W. Tozer; The Practice of the Presence of God by Brother Lawrence; Hearing God by Dallas Willard; and Celebration of Discipline by Richard Foster.
[98] Hebrews 12:2
[99] I owe this illustration to John Ortberg, The Life You've Always Wanted. Pages 55-56.
[100] Exodus 3

Chapter 5
[101] Luke 23:6-12
[102] Luke 15:11-32

[103] Luke 10:25-37
[104] Bonhoeffer, Dietrich. The Cost of Discipleship.
[105] Bonhoeffer, Dietrich. The Cost of Discipleship. Pages 43-56.
[106] Matthew 10:39
[107] Luke 9:23
[108] Luke 14:26
[109] Matthew 19:21
[110] John 17:20-23
[111] In his book, Simplify Your Life and Get More Out Of It, H. Norman Wright challenges Christians to scale back so that they can focus on what is truly important. I would suggest that scaling back can allow us more freedom to be still in God's presence.
[112] John 14:15
[113] Matthew 28:20
[114] Luke 11:28
[115] John 15:14
[116] James 1:22-25
[117] Matthew 3:2
[118] John 8:11
[119] Romans 12:1
[120] Psalm 24:1
[121] Hebrews 13:5
[122] Author Unknown. I found this poem in Tim Hansel's book, Holy Sweat. Pages 51-53.

Chapter 6
[123] Ephesians 2:1-10
[124] In his book, Not the Way It's Supposed to Be, Cornelius Plantinga describes sin as a "vandalism of shalom." Pages 7-27.
[125] Romans 7:7-24
[126] Hebrews 4:15
[127] Luke 22:42
[128] Matthew 5:48
[129] Romans 8:38-39

[130] 2 Corinthians 3:18
[131] Lewis, C.S. Mere Christianity. Page 167. I owe thanks to Rev. Adam Barton, a pastor in the Christian Reformed Church, for pointing out this reference.
[132] Romans 7:5
[133] Titus 3:3
[134] Galatians 5:24
[135] Romans 1:18-32
[136] Matthew 6:13
[137] Matthew 5:30
[138] Chamber, Oswald. My Utmost For His Highest. June 29
[139] Galatians 5:17
[140] Philippians 3:12-14. In Paul's epistles, he frequently uses the image of running a race (1 Corinthians 9:24-26, Galatians 2:2, 5:7, Philippians 2:16, 2 Timothy 4:7). In these passages it becomes evident that following Christ is like an endurance race. It is not something we complete quickly. It requires patience and training. Followers will face many obstacles.
[141] Most of my reflection on the problem of hypocrisy stems from the writings of Cornelius Plantinga, Jr., president of Calvin Theological Seminary. I highly recommend his book, Not The Way It's Supposed to Be: A Breviary of Sin (pages 96-113), and his article in the February 2004 issue of The Banner, "Hypocrisy and Grace: A Meditation for Lent."
[142] 1 John 1:8
[143] Psalm 86:11

Chapter 7
[144] Ephesians 5:1
[145] Philippians 2:5
[146] Gatorade launched an advertisement campaign that summer which hinted that people could become more like Michael Jordan if they drank Gatorade. The theme song for this campaign was a catchy tune that repeated the words, "be like Mike."

[147] Luke 9:2
[148] Luke 9:10
[149] Luke 9:13
[150] Luke 9:20
[151] Luke 9:23-27
[152] I use the words Messiah and Christ interchangeably. Christ is the New Testament Greek term that has its equivalent in the Hebrew term Messiah. When Peter said Jesus was the Christ, he was saying that Jesus was the promised Messiah from the Old Testament.
[153] Luke 9:28-36
[154] Luke 9:46-48
[155] Luke 9:49
[156] Luke 9:54
[157] Luke 9:57-62
[158] Isaiah 6:5
[159] Proverbs 1:7
[160] Genesis 3:15
[161] In his book, Jesus The Jewish Theologian, Brad Young says there is an element of chutzpah, or bold persistence, in true faith. Pages 171-180.
[162] Genesis 18:16-33. This passage is the story of Abraham pleading for Sodom and Gomorrah.
[163] Numbers 14 tells the story of Israel's rebellion and Moses' intervention on their behalf.
[164] Matthew 15:21-28
[165] Philippians 2:5-8. The quote was only verse 5, but the rest of the text goes on to describe how Christ emptied Himself and worked from a position of humility.
[166] John 13:1-20
[167] Luke 23:34
[168] Matthew 6:12
[169] Lewis, C.S. Mere Christianity. Pages 160-166. Lewis uses the word pretend as I am using the word imitate. He does not mean to challenge us to manage our image for others, but to experience transformation as we imitate.

[170] Luke 14:7-11
[171] Philippians 2:9-11

Chapter 8

[172] The Karate Kid. Written by Robert Mark Kamen and directed by John G. Avildsen. Ralph Macchio starred as Daniel LaRusso, and Noriyuku "Pat" Morita as Mr. Kesuke Miyagi. Columbia/Tristar Studios, 1984.
[173] John 14:2
[174] Leviticus 19:2, Matthew 5:48
[175] Deuteronomy 30:6
[176] These categories are wonderfully explained The Book of Leviticus, by Gordon J. Wenham in the section titled "The Theology of Leviticus." Pages 15-32.
[177] Deuteronomy 5:48
[178] 2 Corinthians 3:18
[179] In his book, Mere Christianity, C.S. Lewis has an entire chapter on becoming new creatures in Christ entitled, "Nice Creatures or New Men." Pages 175-183.
[180] Acts 15:21
[181] 1 Corinthians 9:25
[182] 1 Timothy 4:7-8
[183] 2 Timothy 3:16-17
[184] Romans 12:2
[185] Yancey, Philip. Reaching for The Invisible God. Pages 202-208.
[186] 1 Thessalonians 5:17
[187] John 3:8
[188] 1 Corinthians 3
[189] Augustine. Confessions. Pages 153-154.
[190] 2 Corinthians 12:7
[191] Acts 8:3. In this passage, he was still referred to as Saul. Prior to Acts 13, Paul is referred to as Saul. Acts 13:9 explains that he was also known as Paul, and for the remainder of the book of Acts, he is called Paul.

[192] Saul's conversion story is found in Acts 9.
[193] 1 Corinthians 15:58
[194] In his book Union With Christ Lewis Smedes describes salvation as the combination of three things: Christ in us, and we both in and with Him.
[195] Matthew 18:20

Chapter 9
[196] 1 Corinthians 4:16
[197] Hebrews 6:12, 13:7
[198] John 14:12
[199] In the beginning of Eugene Peterson's book, Subversive Spirituality, Peterson tells a story of his young grandson playing with a tennis ball, and then forgetting about the ball once it rolls out of sight. Pages 16-17.
[200] John 14:15-31
[201] I realize that in the Roman Catholic Church, the position of the pope can be traced back to the Apostle Peter. However, the position of pope was never intended to be a replacement for Christ. In fact, the pope is considered the bishop of Rome, the leader of many bishops, who are called to continue the ministry of Christ's church.
[202] Matthew 28:19
[203] Jesus instructed Peter to "feed my lambs," and "take care of my sheep" in John 21:15-16.
[204] 1 Kings 18
[205] Elijah twice said that he was all alone. 1 Kings 19:10,14
[206] Acts 2:42-47
[207] John 17:20-21
[208] Hebrews 10:25
[209] "Conjunction Junction." ABC Schoolhouse Rock (1973). Music and Lyrics by Bob Dorough. Performed by Jack Sheldon. Animation by Phil Kimmelman and Associates.
[210] Proverbs 27:17
[211] Romans 12:10

[212] Romans 12:16
[213] Romans 14:13
[214] Romans 15:7
[215] 1 Corinthians 16:20
[216] Galatians 5:13
[217] Galatians 6:2
[218] Ephesians 4:2
[219] Ephesians 4:32
[220] Ephesians 5:21
[221] Colossians 3:9
[222] 1 Thessalonians 4:9
[223] 1 Thessalonians 5:11
[224] 1 Thessalonians 5:13
[225] Titus 2
[226] Matthew 7:1-5
[227] John 17:20-21

Chapter 10
[228] Matthew 14:22-36
[229] Luke 22:33
[230] Matthew 16:22-23
[231] John 18:10-11
[232] Culpepper, R. Alan. Anatomy of the Fourth Gospel. Page 123.
[233] Mark 9:5
[234] Acts 2:14-41
[235] Matthew 16:16
[236] Peter means rock in Greek.
[237] 2 Samuel 12
[238] Judges 13-14. Samson was supposed to be a Nazirite, which meant he could not drink wine, cut his hair, nor come near a dead body (Numbers 6:1-8). Samson violated all of these standards.
[239] Acts 20:9
[240] Genesis 37
[241] 2 Kings 5:8-10

[242] Numbers 20:1-13
[243] John 12:4 tells a story of Judas pretending concern for the poor, when in fact, he was concerned about money. He had charge of the money within the group of Jesus' followers.
[244] John 13:12-17
[245] Matthew 16:22
[246] Luke 9:33
[247] John 18:10
[248] Matthew 26:33
[249] Matthew 26:69-75
[250] John 15:14
[251] John 21
[252] John 21:17
[253] John 21:15-17
[254] John 21:19,22. Even when Peter became distracted and asked about the status of another disciple, Jesus spoke in a way to help Peter remember that his primary focus was supposed to be on following Him.
[255] Acts 5 tells of the apostles being persecuted. Acts 12 tells of Peter being imprisoned.
[256] 1 Peter 2:13
[257] 1 Peter 3:14

Chapter 11
[258] Matthew 4:21
[259] Matthew 10:2
[260] John 13:23
[261] John 20:1-9
[262] Matthew 20:20-28
[263] Mark 10:35-45
[264] Luke 9:51-55
[265] John 13:23-25
[266] John 19:25-35
[267] John 20:2-10
[268] John 21:20-21

[269] Luke 14:8-11
[270] John 19:25-27
[271] John 20:1-9
[272] John 20:8
[273] John 13:24
[274] Mark 9:38, Luke 9:49, Mark 10:35, Mark 13:3, Luke 9:54, John 13:3, John 21:7
[275] Mark 5:37 tells the story of Jesus taking only Peter, James, and John with him when He performed a miracle. Peter, James, and John were witness to many incidents that the other disciples did not observe.
[276] Luke 2:19
[277] Luke 10:38-42
[278] Psalm 46:10
[279] Matthew 14:23
[280] John 19:25-27
[281] Kempis, Thomas a'. The Imitation of Christ. Page 76.
[282] Revelation 1:9

Chapter 12

[283] John 20:25
[284] Mark 16:14
[285] Luke 24:26-43
[286] John 20:28
[287] Culpepper, R. Alan. The Anatomy of the Fourth Gospel. Page 123.
[288] Matthew 10:3, Mark 3:18, Luke 6:15
[289] John 11:16
[290] John 14:5
[291] John 14:6
[292] John 14:8
[293] John 20:24-29
[294] John 11:16
[295] John 14:5
[296] John 20:26
[297] 2 Corinthians 12:8-9 is an example of Paul praying three times for

his "thorn" to be removed, which did not happen.
[298] Job 1-2
[299] Mark 8:34
[300] Romans 8:38-39
[301] Nehemiah 8:10
[302] Philippians 4:13
[303] Isaiah 40:31
[304] Psalm 13:1
[305] Psalm 22:1
[306] Psalm 88:18
[307] 1 Samuel 13:14, 1 Kings 11:4
[308] Matthew 11:28
[309] Job 42:7
[310] John 20:24-31
[311] John 20:30-31
[312] John 20:29

Chapter 13
[313] John 2:1-11
[314] John 4:43-54
[315] John 5:1-15
[316] John 6:1-15
[317] John 6:14-15,24
[318] John 6:26-27
[319] John 6:53
[320] John 6:60
[321] John 6:66
[322] John 6:70
[323] John 12:6
[324] John 13:1-17
[325] John 12:1-11
[326] John 18:2
[327] John 12:5
[328] Judas objected to the anointing of Christ in John 12. Peter objected

to Christ's prediction of suffering in Mark 8:32.
[329] John 21
[330] Matthew 26:24
[331] Matthew 26:21, Mark 14:17-21, Luke 22:20, John 13:21
[332] Matthew 26:33-34, Mark 14:29-30, Luke 22:33-34, John 13:37-38
[333] Matthew 26:14-16, Mark 14:10-11, Luke 22:3-6
[334] Matthew 26:74
[335] Luke 9:23
[336] Deuteronomy 6:4-9
[337] Matthew 26:69-27:5 tells the stories of Peter and Judas responding to their actions.
[338] John 21:15-19
[339] Matthew 26:75
[340] Matthew 27:3
[341] Luke 23:34
[342] Yancey, Philip. What's So Amazing About Grace? Page 180.

Chapter 14
[343] Acts 1:15
[344] Some scholars believe that John Mark was the author of the gospel of Mark, and that he identified his relationship with Jesus in Mark 14:51-52. In that passage, a young man runs away from the scene of Jesus' arrest while he is naked.
[345] Paul is widely recognized as the author of Romans, 1 and 2 Corinthians, Galatians, Ephesians, Philippians, Colossians, 1 and 2 Thessalonians, 1 and 2 Timothy, Titus, and Philemon.
[346] Early in the book of Acts, Paul is identified as Saul. In Acts 13:9 we are told that he was known by both names.
[347] Acts 8:1
[348] Acts 8:2
[349] Acts 22:3
[350] Philippians 3:4-6
[351] Acts 16:37
[352] 1 Corinthians 15:9

[353] 1 Samuel 16:1-13
[354] Joshua 2
[355] 1 Samuel 3
[356] Kregel, Jon. Dealer.
[357] Lewis, C.S. Surprised By Joy: The Shape of My Early Life.
[358] Colson, Charles W. Born Again.
[359] Augustine, Saint. Confessions.
[360] See Chapter 1
[361] Romans 8:29-30, Ephesians 1:5,11
[362] Romans 8:38-39
[363] Exodus 3
[364] Judges 6
[365] 1 Samuel 3
[366] Mark 12:29-31
[367] Micah 6:8
[368] Acts 9:15
[369] Acts 16:6-10
[370] Apostle means one who is sent out.
[371] Acts 9:13-14, 21, 26
[372] 1 Corinthians 15:8-9
[373] 2 Corinthians 11:5, 12:11
[374] 1 Corinthians 1:31
[375] Acts 1:21-22
[376] Acts 6:1-7

Chapter 15
[377] Ephesians 1:11-12
[378] Acts 8:26-40
[379] Acts 1:26
[380] 2 Corinthians 9:13
[381] 1 Thessalonians 2:6
[382] Mark 5:37
[383] Acts 12:2
[384] Psalm 30:5

[385] Acts 8
[386] Acts 12
[387] Acts 15:7
[388] John 13:12-17
[389] 1 Corinthians 15:58

Chapter 16

[390] Exodus 14
[391] I owe the comparison between discipleship and military service to Dr. Stan Mast, a minister in the Christian Reformed Church.
[392] In his article, "Becoming a Fully Devoted Disciple of Jesus" (Banner, March, 2004), Sid Couperus describes a five step approach that Jesus used to develop His disciples.
[393] John 2:1-11
[394] John 4:43-5:15
[395] Luke 9:13-16
[396] Luke 9:1, 10:1
[397] Matthew 28:16-20
[398] Jeremiah 29:11-14
[399] 2 Corinthians 3:18